PRESENTING AT WORK

A Guide to Public Speaking
in Professional Contexts

CHRISTINE CLAPP and
BJØRN F. STILLION SOUTHARD

Presenting at Work: A Guide to Public Speaking in Professional Contexts

Publisher's Cataloging-in-Publication
(Provided by Quality Books, Inc.)

    Clapp, Christine.
      Presenting at work : a guide to public speaking in
    professional contexts / Christine Clapp and Bjørn F.
    Stillion Southard.
      pages cm
      Includes bibliographical references.
      LCCN 2014915496
      ISBN 978-0-578-14435-1

      1. Business presentations. 2. Public speaking.
    I. Stillion Southard, Bjørn F. II. Title.

    HF5718.22.C53 2014   658.4'52
                  QBI14-600154

Library of Congress Control Number: 2014915496

ISBN 9780578144351 (paperback)
2014—First Edition
Printed in the United States of America

Editing | Allie Benjamin
Additional Editorial Work | Wm. R. "Mac" McKenney
Cover and Interior Design | Melissa Tenpas —www.MelissaTenpas.com
Cover Photography | iStockPhoto® (front) and Elizabeth Dranitzke (back)

TABLE OF CONTENTS

1 Introduction   5

PART I: How You Say It
2 Manage Nervousness   11
3 Overview of the Five S's   19
4 Stance   23
5 Sound   29
6 Smile   35
7 Silence   41
8 Sight   47
9 Modes of Speaking   51

PART II: What You Say
10 Ethics   57
11 Outlining Speeches and the Sandwich Structure   63
12 Analyzing the Situation and Audience   73
13 Topic Selection   79
14 General Purpose and Thesis   85
15 Research   93
16 Supporting Material and Sources of Information   99
17 Storytelling   107
18 Main Points   111
19 Signposting and Transitions   117
20 Attention Getters and Clinchers   123
21 Complementing with PowerPoint and Presentation Aids   131

PART III: Where You Say It
22 Rehearsals   141
23 Briefings and Informative Speeches   149
24 Training Programs and Lectures   155
25 Persuasive Speeches and Pitches   159
26 Meetings   167
27 Teleconferences, Videoconferences, and Webinars   175
28 Panel Moderation and Group Presentations   183
29 Introducing a Speaker   191
30 Question & Answer and Impromptu Speaking   195
31 Job Interviews   201
32 Networking and Social Events   207
33 Evaluations and Performance Appraisals   213
34 Award Ceremonies   217
35 Toasts   223
36 Speeches to Inspire   227
37 After Dinner Speaking   231
38 Unexpected Places to Gain Speaking Experience   235

PART IV: What Next
39 Concluding Remarks and How to Continue Improving   239

APPENDICES   241
I   Sample Outlines for Various Occasions   245
II   Recover from a Disappointing Presentation   248
III Impromptu Speech Topics   254
IV   Annotated List of Useful Websites for Public Speakers   257
V   Additional Resources on Presenting and Speechwriting   262

ACKNOWLEDGEMENTS   263

─────── CHAPTER 1 ───────

INTRODUCTION

When Apple released its first iMac, iPhone, and iPad, the company turned to its CEO, Steve Jobs, to deliver the pitch. In rooms that over the years grew larger and more populated, Jobs strode onto the stage wearing his signature round spectacles, black turtleneck, and light blue jeans—and spoke about the new innovations of his cutting-edge company. In an age dominated by electronic communication technology, Jobs turned to speaking—the oldest of communication technologies—to launch their products.

When an April 2010 explosion on the offshore *Deepwater Horizon* oil-drilling rig owned by British Petroleum (BP) killed 11 men and injured 17 others, not to mention, threatened the environment and the economy of the Gulf of Mexico, the public demanded accountability from the company's executives. A press release would not suffice. The face and voice of the BP's senior-most executives—notably BP's then-Chief Executive Tony Hayward—were called upon to deliver statements about what caused the explosion and subsequent oil spill, when it would be fixed, how the Gulf would be restored, and how future catastrophes would be prevented. In such moments of crisis, businesses like BP turn to their leadership to speak to address the issues, to apologize for suffering, and ideally to help resolve problems.

When President Bill Clinton stood before a joint session of Congress in 1993, prepared to deliver the first major policy speech of his presidency on healthcare, his hallmark issue, the assembled audience and the millions at home expected polish, poise, and persuasion. What no one knew was that the wrong speech had been loaded on the president's TelePrompTer (the electronic device that was supposed to display the text of his remarks). For seven minutes the president spoke extemporaneously, glancing, on occasion, at the correct paper version of the speech in front of him. Those seven minutes, according to his pollsters, registered unusually high favorability ratings. At an incredibly significant moment in Clinton's first year in office, he relied upon his skill and preparation as a public speaker to overcome a potential political disaster.[1]

The examples above concern high-level leaders in extraordinary situations, which might invite some readers to question whether public speaking is relevant for most professionals and a worthy area of study for students. Do I really need to know how to speak publicly? That kind of thing won't happen to me, will it? Well, those are good questions and an important starting point for this text.

Our response to your question comes in the form of another question: **Do you want to develop the communication skills necessary to advance your career, hold positions of leadership, or solve pressing problems?**

If you answered "yes," keep reading for help developing those skills. If you answered "no," keep reading and let us convince you otherwise.

Just ask Emily Murphy about the importance of public speaking. The managing editor of Mother Nature Network (www.mnn.com), a website that provides green content and breaking environmental news. Early in her time at MNN, Emily was asked to speak on a panel at an industry conference. When called upon for remarks, her heart was racing, breathing was difficult, and her voice faltered. Though she got through the presentation, Emily wasn't proud of her performance.

After the panel, she was mortified when an audience member approached her and told her she could really improve by joining his Toastmasters Club, a chapter of the internationally renowned public-speaking organization. The experience motivated her to develop her presentation skills. After all, it was her responsibility to pitch prospective sponsors to raise funds, and to speak at journalism and green businesses conferences to raise awareness of MNN and bolster its reputation. Without honing her public speaking skills, Emily would be letting down MNN and its mission to improve both the environment and the lives of readers.

And ask Leonardo Goncalves about the role public speaking plays in career success. After working in finance at several corporations, Leo, a native of Brazil who studied business at The Wharton School of the University of Pennsylvania, became a manager at Deloitte Consulting in the Washington, D.C. metro area. After five years serving clients in that role, he had an opportunity to advance to senior manager. To win the coveted promotion, he had to go through a rigorous selection process, culminating in a one-hour PowerPoint presentation to a regional panel of partners at Deloitte that covered his background, experience, value to the company, and vision for bringing in future business. Just like a job interview, it was a high-stakes, make-or-break presentation. Leo used stories to connect with the panel and make his pitch stand out from his competition. His strategy worked—he landed the senior manager position and catapulted his career.

NO MATTER YOUR CAREER PATH, STRONG COMMUNICATION SKILLS ARE ALWAYS IN DEMAND.

Take it from Emily and Leo: No matter your career path, strong communication skills always are in demand. If you need more proof, read through job announcements in your field or intended career field. It is hard to find positions that don't require strong oral communication skills. And for empirical evidence, look to the study that found communication skills were ranked as the most important qualities employers seek, ahead of even computer skills and a strong work ethic.[2]

Communication skills become more important as one takes on new professional responsibilities. A 2007 study showed that demands to speak in front of groups of various sizes increase as one rises through the corporate ranks: New hires spend 25% of their time in meetings, middle managers spend 50%, and top executives present or listen in meetings 75% of their time.[3]

Beyond speaking in meetings, crises and opportunities arise in organizations big and small that demand a leader to rise to the occasion. And *anyone* (presidents included) can forget to bring the right draft of a speech, lose his or her train of thought mid presentation, or have PowerPoint slides that just won't load correctly. Preparing for and managing professional speaking moments are skills worth developing—and ones that will set you apart from colleagues and competitors who have not mastered the art of communicating with confidence.

EMERGING TECHNOLOGIES ALSO HAVE CREATED A NEED FOR PUBLIC SPEAKING SKILLS THAT ADDRESS THE CURRENT COMMUNICATION ENVIRONMENT.

Emerging technologies also have created a need for public speaking skills that address the current communication environment. Many of these new technologies facilitate increased oral communication. For example, Skype, FaceTime, Webex, GoToMeeting, and other video chat or video conferencing technologies have expanded the possibilities for presentations across distances. The presence of such technologies on computers, tablets, and mobile phones eliminates nearly all constraints to participating in (virtual) face-to-face reports, presentations, and meetings. Knowing how to present using these and other technologies are 21st century public speaking skills that must be learned and practiced.

And with so much mediated communication, the demand for meaningful face-to-face encounters has only increased. Imagine a situation in which you are one of many division managers in a company. When all managers are asked to deliver a report, observed for a performance appraisal, or interviewed for a promotion, do you want to stand out? Do you want to look and sound like a person who can only function using txt msgs? ORLY? U do? Delivering presentations in a polished and professional manner will only complement other communication skills that you use in a professional setting.

This book provides the tools you need to meet the demands of public speaking in a professional context—from networking and job interviewing to formal presentations and special occasion speeches. Whether you're in college and preparing for a professional career, just beginning your career and looking for ways to advance, ascending through the ranks and taking on new responsibilities, or searching for new ways to energize your speaking, this handbook will help.

Calling this text a handbook is indicative of our overall approach. We want the information to be easily accessible and helpful at multiple stages of one's professional development. We want this text to be something you can easily turn to for reference and ideas. We do not want it riddled with stock photos of people giving speeches or other filler that increases the weight and cost of the book but not its utility.

To those ends, we have divided the text in three sections. Part I covers *How You Say It*. This section of book addresses issues related to effectively delivering your message. Part II addresses *What You Say*. This section delivers important information and useful tools for structuring your presentation in a clear and meaningful way. Part III covers *Where You Say It*. This section focuses on how to successfully manage a variety of speech situations you may encounter in the professional world.

The chapters contained within these sections are swiftly presented, providing practical information and useful exercises. We have chosen to limit theoretical discussions within the text, including it only where practically applicable and providing an occasional footnote for those who are interested in pursuing certain topics more deeply. This choice comes from years of talking to professional clients about their needs within a business context and working with career-bound undergraduates.

Perhaps the greatest virtue of the handbook is that it addresses topics not often found in corporate communications books or conveyed upon landing a new job or promotion: How do I give a toast? How do I run a meeting? How do I organize a successful conference panel? How do I conduct a training program or webinar? How do I pitch an idea at a networking event or to my manager during a two-minute elevator ride? We address these topics and more because these are the realities of the professional world.

The communication environment is rapidly changing, but the importance of public speaking remains. Ultimately, we hope to provide the skills to adapt this environment, to rise to the occasion, and, most importantly, to speak with authority. ∎

---

1. For a fuller account of this story, see Johnson, Haynes and David S. Broder. *The System: The American Way of Politics and the Breaking Point.* New York: Little, Brown and Co, 1996. Print.

2. "Job Outlook 2012". *National Association of Colleges and Employers.* 26 Oct. 2011. Web. 16 Oct. 2013.

3. Souter, Nick. *Persuasive Presentations: How to Get the Response You Need.* New York: Sterling Publishing, 2007. Print.

—————— CHAPTER 2 ——————

HOW YOU SAY IT
Manage Nervousness

Mark Twain once said, "There are two types of speakers: those that are nervous and those that are liars." And, to a large extent, research backs up this old saw.

Take for example, the famous 1973 survey by R.H. Bruskin Associates. It showed that of 2,543 American men and women, the fear of public speaking ranked higher than their fear of heights, insects and bugs, and even death.

This chapter aims to equip speakers with strategies for managing nervousness, including having realistic expectations, putting presentations in perspective, preparing for success, and channeling nervous energy into enthusiasm.

HAVE REALISTIC EXPECTATIONS

For the vast majority of speakers, rehearsal and experience will reduce, but not eliminate, the jitters associated with giving a speech. If you happen to be in the small minority of speakers whose anxiety gets significantly worse and not incrementally better with each exposure to public speaking, you should discuss the problem with your doctor and get a medical assessment. There are treatments and medications available for people diagnosed with a social anxiety disorder. But such extreme cases are extremely rare.

Trying to eliminate nervousness associated with presenting only makes it worse. Instead, expect and accept that you'll be nervous. Then, focus your attention on channeling nervous energy into positive energy during your presentation with memorable expressions, gestures, and vocal variety.

Even the most seasoned and celebrated speakers get nervous—just talk to the president before his State of the Union Address or a business leader before unveiling a new product. Nervous speakers can give great speeches; peg your success on other factors, such as winning a new client or closing a sale, changing audience attitudes toward a subject, or receiving positive feedback on evaluation forms or a performance review.

PUT IT IN PERSPECTIVE

Remember, it is just a speech. It is not a life-or-death situation, as much as we like to make it out to be at times. Think through the worst-case scenario—tripping as you walk to the lectern, forgetting what you were planning to say, getting a question that you can't answer off the top of your head, or having a heckler in your audience. While not ideal, the worst-case scenario usually is not that bad. And you can make a contingency plan for dealing with such scenarios to put your mind at ease. For example, prepare a quip to say if you do happen to trip on the way to the lectern; craft an outline that allows you to get back on message if you lose your train of thought; practice a "thanks-for-your-question-and-I'll-have-to-get-back-to-you-on-that" response for times when audience members stump you during Q&A; or identify strategies to disarm detractors and win the respect of other audience members.

Also, remember not to be your own worst critic. There is no such thing as a perfect speech. Don't aim for perfection; aim for your best. Chances are audience members won't notice when things don't go quite according to plan. Presenters often assume that audience members are picking out small flaws like a mispronounced word or a typo on a slide. They aren't—listeners either care for you or just don't care. A much bigger issue than critical audience members is distracted ones. Like most of us, technological gadgets and thoughts of what's for dinner are competing for attention.

PRESENTERS OFTEN ASSUME THAT AUDIENCE MEMBERS ARE PICKING OUT SMALL FLAWS LIKE A MISPRONOUNCED WORD OR A TYPO ON A SLIDE. THEY AREN'T.

Even when you do keep listeners engaged, they likely won't notice hiccups in your speech unless you point them out with disclaimers (like apologizing that your voice is hoarse) or showing signs of frustration (like furrowing your brow or muttering a side comment about a problem with the technology).

In fact, people in your audience generally want you to succeed. They don't want to waste time by sitting through a presentation that stinks; they don't want to waste money by attending a workshop or conference that doesn't contain useful information; and, they certainly don't want to feel nervous or embarrassed for a speaker who is struggling at the lectern.

PREPARE FOR SUCCESS

In addition to setting realistic expectations for your presentation and putting speeches in perspective, you can also prepare for success at the lectern.

IN THE LONG-TERM, DEVELOP YOUR PRESENTATION SKILLS:

- Take advantage of opportunities to speak and get feedback—in class, at work, and though organizations like Toastmasters International, which is a renowned network of clubs dedicated to helping members become better public speakers.

- Use everyday encounters to become a better speaker. If you know you tend to speak softly, focus on belting out your order at your favorite coffee shop. Or if you punctuate your speaking with "ums" and "ahs," take care to avoid such words when catching up with a friend over dinner.

IN THE MID-TERM, WHEN YOU KNOW YOU HAVE AN UPCOMING PRESENTATION

- Block adequate time on your calendar for the process of crafting and rehearsing material (at least a month for a major speech and a week for a short or informal presentation).

- Practice at least six times, and record and review your later rehearsals.

- Consider hiring a coach to guide and advise you through the process.

IN THE SHORT-TERM, ON THE DAY OF A PRESENTATION:

- Run through your pre-speaking routine. A pre-speaking routine gets you ready mentally and physically to perform at your best on the day of your important presentation. Just like elite athletes who follow a careful routine for eating, hydrating, dressing, focusing, stretching, and warming up on the morning of an important race or match, a public speaker shouldn't overlook these important elements that contribute to peak performance, whether they're interviewing for a job, pitching a client, moderating a panel, toasting a friend's success, or keynoting at a conference.

It takes trial and error to identify what helps you speak at your best. But consider the following elements when you develop your pre-speaking routine for the first time.

FUEL

Foods you eat on the day of a presentation should provide energy; they shouldn't slow you down or threaten to upset your stomach. Play with the timing of the last meal or snack you eat before your presentation. And don't forget fluids. Avoid drinking caffeinated beverages right before going on stage, as they can make you too jittery. And caffeine can stress the vocal chords, as can hot and cold beverages. It is better to hydrate with room-temperature water starting at least one day before a presentation. If you chug water right before going on stage, you might find yourself focusing more on the location of the restroom than connecting with your audience.

MENTAL EXERCISES

No amount of rehearsal will result in an excellent performance if you don't believe in yourself. That's why it's so important to focus mentally before a speech. Every speaker will have methods that work to get his or her head in the game in the hours leading up to a presentation. Yours might include listening to special music, reading inspirational quotations, practicing relaxation techniques, visualizing speaking success, or running through your presentation (in part or in its entirety).

PHYSICAL EXERCISES

You may not be participating in an elite athletic event, but public speaking is a physical activity. Vernon Jordan once said about delivering a speech, "You're supposed to be exhausted when you're done."

In order to perform at your peak, it's important to warm up the muscles of your body and voice beforehand. Consider exercising the morning of your presentation or taking a brisk walk shortly before it is set to begin. Do some stretches you've learned through participation in a sport or activity like yoga. Focus especially on loosening up the shoulders, chest, neck, and jaw—all areas where speakers commonly carry tension. And don't forget to warm up your mouth (by blowing air through your lips), your jaw (by yawning), and your voice (by saying the following tongue twisters, and any of your own favorites, five times in a loud, slow, and clear voice).

- Red leather, yellow leather
- Blue leather, black leather
- Dig a big pig
- Sushi chef

- Giggle gaggle
- Unique New York
- Toy boat
- All I want is a proper pot of coffee, made in a proper copper coffee pot.

CHANNEL NERVOUS ENERGY INTO ENTHUSIASM

Rather than worrying about getting rid of butterflies in your stomach, channel your nervous energy into the elements of dynamic speech delivery: vocal variations, facial expressions, and body movements.

First, project your voice so it fills the room with sound. Use occasional increases and decreases in volume to add excitement or suspense to your speech. Also, consider varying the pace of your speaking and the pitch of your voice to add interest.

Second, remember to smile during your presentation. Most speakers don't because they are nervous. Smiling won't come across to audience members as silly or cheesy. Flashing your pearly whites throughout your speech conveys confidence and enthusiasm, and builds rapport. Also, exaggerate facial expressions, especially when telling stories, to convey to your audience feelings such as shock, anger, excitement, bewilderment, disappointment, or disgust. This adds meaning to the words you say and helps keep audience members engaged.

Lastly, gesture with your hands to emphasize important points (e.g., counting main ideas on your fingers or pounding one fist into your other palm while repeating a key phrase) and show what you're talking about (e.g., re-enacting how you made the winning shot at a basketball game). You can also walk from one side of your speaking area to the other in order to compliment your verbal transition from one main idea in your presentation to the next. Consider using a prop or other visual aids to give your hands something useful to do. Such purposeful movements will replace repetitive and / or distracting gestures that are manifestations of nervous energy.

Mark Twain was right: Nervousness comes with the territory of public

REMEDIES FOR COMMON SYMPTOMS OF NERVOUSNESS

Butterflies and Upset Stomach

Watch what you eat before you present. Eat bland foods, like a banana or a bagel, and stick to room-temperature water. Make sure to have medicine on hand to treat an upset stomach–just in case!

Racing Heart and Rapid Breathing

There is a simple way to help slow a racing heart and rapid breathing: deep-breathing. Take a slow, sustained breath in to the count of four; fill your lungs and entire chest cavity with air. Then, in a slow and controlled fashion, exhale to the count of five. Repeat as necessary.

Turning Red in the Face

You can't necessarily prevent your cheeks from turning red, but you can avoid wearing reds and oranges, colors that will highlight the redness. Go with colors on the opposite side of the color wheel that de-emphasize blushing, like greens and blues.

Hands that Shake

If your hands tend to shake, avoid holding notes or visual aids. Keep notes on the lectern and project graphs, pictures, etc. on a screen so you can refer to them and not have to hold papers that will shake noticeably.

Voice that Quivers

Speak loudly. The softer you speak, the more your voice can waver. If you focus on using a booming voice and filling the room with sound, you'll find that your voice has much less quiver to it.

speaking. But it doesn't have to cripple your presentations. You can manage nerves by being realistic in your expectations, putting presentations in perspective, and preparing for success. And, practice channeling nervous energy into enthusiasm in your presentation though your use of the elements of dynamic speech delivery.

EXERCISE

Write down a pre-speaking routine, noting the specific activity you will do and when you will do it. Go through it before your next presentation and take note of what you did and when you did it. After the presentation, reflect on the elements of your pre-speaking routine. Was your routine practical? If not, how could you modify it to increase the chances that you will use it in the future? How effective was your routine in lowering your level of nervousness? Are there other elements that you should add? Elements that you should refine, adjust the timing of, or eliminate? Edit your pre-speaking routine in preparation for your next presentation accordingly.

ACTIVITY

Interview someone who has mastered an activity that you consider nerve-racking (think broadly here, you might speak to someone who launched his or her own business, who has been skydiving, who traveled abroad without an itinerary, etc.). What does he or she do to manage anxiety? How has his or her level of nervousness and coping strategies changed over time? How did he or she feel after taking on or mastering a nerve-racking activity? How will you apply what you learned from the interviewee to your practice of public speaking? ∎

—— CHAPTER 3 ——

HOW YOU SAY IT
Overview of the 5 S's

Whether you're speaking in the classroom, conference room, or break room, there are five principles of confident delivery: stance, sound, smile, silence, and sight. What follows is an overview of each of these five speaking proficiencies, which will be expanded upon in subsequent chapters.

But first, remember that the goal of speech delivery is to be yourself at your best. Describing best practices of confident presentations should in no way be taken as an invitation or recommendation that you take on the persona of a stand-up comic, newscaster, politician, motivational speaker, or businessperson that you (or your listeners) admire. The goal is a delivery style that is both authentic and polished. Here's how you can strike that balance in the five aspects of speaking with confidence.

STANCE

Stand firm and stand tall. Keep your feet planted on the ground about hip-distance apart, with weight equally distributed on the legs. Imagine that your feet have set in concrete to prevent rocking, swaying, tapping, or pacing. Also, keep your hands at your sides in a neutral position rather than "talking with the hands" or making repetitive motions with them at your waist. Purposeless movement distracts listeners from your message and is a sure sign of nervousness.

With your feet grounded, stand tall. Roll your shoulders back and open your chest, expanding the area from your hips to your shoulders. Hold your head high, like there's a string attached from the crown of your head to the ceiling. But make sure your chin is down. Excellent posture conveys confidence before a single word is spoken.

SOUND

With the foundation of excellent posture, you can project by speaking from your diaphragm, not from your throat. This will help you fill the room with sound and also ensure that your voice is grounded—on the low end of its natural range (lowly). Most presenters perceive themselves to be much louder than their audience does. After all, you likely never have left an event thinking: "That speaker was just too loud!" Remember to speak louder than you think you should. The same could be said for rate of delivery: remember to speak slower than you think you should. When speakers are nervous, excited, or anxious to finish, the rate of speaking can increase, making it difficult for listeners to appreciate the message. In sum, the fundamentals of effective vocal delivery are to speak loudly, lowly, and slowly.

SMILE

Show your pearly whites. Smiling not only makes your voice pleasant sounding, it also conveys confidence. Even if you're terrified of public speaking, no one will know if you have a smile on your face. Rest assured, smiling throughout a presentation won't make you look cheesy. You will appear friendly, approachable, and composed. Whenever it's appropriate for your topic (and it usually is), throw on a smile. At times in a presentation when a smile is not appropriate, use other facial expressions to convey emotion. For example, when delivering bad news, your face should show concern or disappointment.

SILENCE

Use . . . long . . . pauses. Most Americans are uncomfortable with silence. This causes speakers to turn sentences into run-ons and to fill pauses with "junk" words, such as "um," "ah," "you know," "kind of," "like," "so," and "well." These fillers make speakers look unpolished, unprepared, and unprofessional. To overcome junk words, start correcting yourself in casual conversations and enlist the help of friends, family members, and colleagues to point out when you slip up.

Additionally, if you lose your train of thought, don't apologize or show any outward signs of frustration. These reactions only draw attention to a mistake. Minimize inevitable stumbles by silently finding your place in your notes or taking a sip of water to regain composure. While such a pause may feel uncomfortable to the speaker, it often goes unnoticed by audience members.

SIGHT

Make lasting eye contact. Hold your gaze on an audience member for three full seconds—much longer than you think you should. Then move on and hold your gaze on someone else in a different part of the room. Sustained and direct eye contact builds rapport by giving audience members the feeling that they are engaged in an intimate conversation.

Avoid scanning the room without stopping to look directly at anyone. Also, avoid making eye contact with just a few people in the room who are nodding, smiling, and paying close attention. Ignore the suggestion of looking at the back of the room rather than your listeners to reduce nervousness. Audience members want you to speak to them, not at them.

Remember the five S's of confident delivery: stance, sound, smile, silence, and sight. If you can master them in your authentic voice, you will convey confidence in every speaking situation.

EXERCISE

Record yourself giving a sample speech (if you do not have an old presentation on hand, go to Appendix III topic ideas). Watch the recording. Write an inventory your speaking skills, playing close attention to the five S's (stance, sound, smile, silence, and sight). What jumped out at you as areas needing improvement? Which proficiencies are your strengths? Based on this analysis, set two specific goals for your next presentation.

ACTIVITY

Watch a recording of a speaker you admire. Inventory his or her speaking skills, again, playing close attention to the five S's. Which proficiencies are strengths of the speaker? Which could he or she improve upon? Did your careful inventory change your evaluation of the speaker? Explain. ▪

———— CHAPTER 4 ————

HOW YOU SAY IT
Stance

To master the art of speaking with confidence, start with your stance. It is the foundation from which habits of effective delivery are built.

After all, you can craft compelling content, but if you're constantly fidgeting during a presentation, you will distract listeners from your message. And if your shoulders are slouching while you speak, you'll come across as insecure no matter how well you know your material.

This chapter offers basic guidelines on stance, starting from the ground and working up. These suggestions aim to avoid distracting movements, convey confidence and authenticity, and support vocal projection.

LOWER BODY

Keep your feet firmly planted on the ground—as if set in concrete. Avoid all pacing, dancing, tapping, crossing of your feet, or rocking up on your toes. Such movements only detract from your message.

Keep your feet planted hip distance apart so the legs aren't too close or too far apart. Legs that are too close together make a speaker appear mousy; legs that are too far apart can look sloppy and awkward. To check that your feet truly are at hip distance, jump in the air. Note where your feet land; this is where they should be positioned during presentations.

Also, avoid popping a hip or shifting weight from one side to the other. At best, such movements are distracting. At worst, they can come across as unprofessional or evoke a "Valley Girl" persona.

Ideally, you should learn to stand still and control your body before adding movement to different parts of your speaking area or the room. This helps ensure that foot movement is purposeful, rather than a distracting manifestation of nervous energy.

But if you have "happy" feet, and struggle to stand in one place while presenting, it might be helpful to move purposefully in the room. For example, you might stand at a lectern for the introduction of your speech, move to the right-hand side of the speaking area to talk about your first main point, walk to the left-hand side of the speaking area while transitioning to the next point, deliver your second main point there, and return to the lectern for your conclusion. This harmonizes your movement with the speech, and subtly cues listeners to the structure of and transitions in your presentation.

HANDS

If you are like many novice presenters, you might wonder what to do with your hands. You should let them hang naturally at your sides, between purposeful and impactful gestures. Though this sounds easy to do, keeping your hands at your sides in a neutral position may not initially feel natural; it can be a real challenge to make this practice a habit.

Many speakers make the mistake of moving their hands in a distracting manner (e.g., repetitive movements at the waist, talking with the hands, tapping fingers on the lectern, or jangling pocket change). These all are manifestations of nervous energy, rather than purposeful movements that add meaning to a presentation. But you might be wondering why the hands should stay at your sides, rather than in other, and perhaps more comfortable positions.

Well, speakers should keep their hands at their sides because it is a neutral position. Other hand placements can have negative connotations. For example, crossing the arms over the chest can convey defensiveness; putting the hands on the hips can come across as bossy or matter-of-fact; placing hands in pants pockets can lead to the clanking of contents or shoulders that are raised too high; clasping the hands in front of the body can be read as nervous, closed off, or insecure; and, holding the hands behind the back can look as if the speaker is trying to hide something. In addition to conveying undesirable or unintended meanings, such positions can prevent speakers from gesturing in purposeful and memorable ways.

KEEPING HANDS HANGING LOOSELY AT THE SIDES LOOKS NEUTRAL AND NATURAL TO AUDIENCE MEMBERS.

Other hand habits to avoid are holding on to the lectern for dear life or resting the hands on a table situated in front of you when a lectern is not available. Both positions prevent the hands from gesturing purposefully, and even more problematically, they can cause the speaker to hunch over, crippling his or her ability to stand confidently and project loudly.

Keeping hands hanging loosely at the sides (and not with a death grip on clothing or thighs) looks neutral and natural to audience members. Initially, this will feel odd, especially to speakers who are in the habit of "talking" with the hands or using repetitive hand gestures to burn nervous energy.

But with some practice, allowing hands to hang naturally at the sides will feel like second nature. It will put an end to distracting movements and will free up the hands and arms for interesting gestures that emphasize points or help paint a picture for the audience.

After you have learned to control your hands and avoid distractions, you are ready to advance to the point of adding purposeful gestures. When gesturing, project confidence and grace by moving slowly, making broad movements, and keeping the fingers together. In general, aim to stay in the "gesture zone," which is roughly from your waist to the bottom of your rib cage, and about shoulders' width across. Gesturing below the waist can appear timid, as though you wanted to gesture, but chickened out. Frequent or rapid gestures can seem frantic or out of control. While a few sweeping and well-timed gestures can add an element of drama to a presentation, aim to keep your purposeful hand movements within your gesture zone.

UPPER BODY

Make sure your shoulders are relaxed and rolled back; they should be as far away from your ears as possible and feel as if you slid them down your shoulder blades. Hunched shoulders signal insecurity, and tense shoulders belie nervousness. Rolling the shoulders back promotes a proud chest, meaning that the chest is both open and lifted. This upper-body posture not only conveys confidence, it also is necessary to project the voice properly from the diaphragm and not from the throat. (See chapter 5 for more on sound.)

And don't forget to stand as tall as possible. One way to achieve this is to imagine that a string attached to the crown of your head is being pulled toward the ceiling. The top of your head should go up, making you stand taller; your chin should go down (as if someone pushed it toward your chest), helping you ground your voice; and you should look straight out at your audience, rather than down your nose at them.

From the soles of your feet to the crown of your head, these guidelines for stance will give you a strong foundation on which to build other speech delivery skills.

KNOW THE DIFFERENCE BETWEEN A LECTERN AND A PODIUM?

All too often used interchangeably, a lectern is a stand used to support a text in a convenient position for a standing speaker, whereas a podium is the platform on which a presenter stands while delivering a speech.

A speaker puts notes on the lectern and stands on the podium. It helps to remember the root word "pod" means foot (as in podiatrist). You put your feet on a podium, not a lectern. A lectern is where you put you put lecture notes.

EXERCISE

Record yourself three times delivering a sample presentation (if you do not have an old presentation on hand, go to Appendix III topic ideas). On the first time through, stand and gesture as you naturally would. On the second, focus on improving your posture and standing still with your hands at your sides in a neutral position throughout the entire story. The third time, maintain your improved posture, add two purposeful and impactful gestures, and keep your hands at your sides in a neutral position between those gestures.

Carefully review the three recordings. What movements did you make in the first recording that might have been distracting to listeners? How successfully were you able to stand completely still in the second? How did your gestures impact the third rendition of your story? How did your stance improve over the three recordings? How can you continue to improve your posture and movements in the future?

ACTIVITY

The next time you are listening to a speaker in a live setting—a presentation, a class, a workshop—draw a diagram of the room. Every minute or so, draw an X where the speaker is located in the room. How did the speaker utilize his or her speaking area? How did the speaker's movement in the room impact his or her ability to convey a message to the audience? If there were elements constraining the location of the speaker, did the speaker adapt well? How can you apply what you learned in this analysis to your next presentation? ▪

CHAPTER 5

HOW YOU SAY IT
Sound

Maya Angelou once said, "Words mean more than what is set down on paper. It takes the human voice to infuse them with shades of deeper meaning."

And that's the speaker's challenge when it comes to sound—making the most of his or her vocal instrument. Here are three ways to convey confidence and add interest with your voice:

VOLUME

First and foremost, speakers must project. If you aren't heard, your message won't get across, nor will any "shades of deeper meaning," for that matter.

Always speak louder than you think you should. Speaking loudly is a sign of confidence. Even in a one-on-one job interview, meeting, or in a situation when you have a microphone available, use a louder volume than you would in an everyday conversation. This ensures that your voice is forceful, that it doesn't quiver, and that it doesn't come across as weak or mousy.

And as the room and audience get larger, your volume must scale up as well. When you are speaking in a conference room or classroom and don't have access to a microphone, you should be speaking in a raised voice, almost yelling, and should feel the sound of your voice resonating in your upper chest. Your voice will feel tired after projecting in this manner; make sure to drink plenty of water and rest your voice before and after such speaking situations.

To project effectively, work on opening up your chest and midsection; stand tall, lift your chest, and roll your shoulders back and down the shoulder blades. Think of filling the entire room with sound—you might visualize your voice as red paint that you are trying to spray on the back wall of the room in which you are presenting. When you project your voice, focus on speaking from the diaphragm, not the throat (this prevents damage to your vocal chords). You should feel sound vibrating in your upper chest and it should require a significant amount of effort to speak loudly.

PRONUNCIATION

Be careful to say words in the generally accepted pattern of sounds and rhythm. Below is a list of commonly mispronounced words in Standard American English:

Word	Incorrect
Nuclear	Nucular
Library	Libarry
February	Febuary
Ask	Axe
Supposedly	Supposably
Especially	Expecially
Often	Often (the T is silent)

PITCH

To project effectively, you must ground your voice—or speak in a pitch that is low and rich. Every voice has its own natural range, and every speaker should aim to speak at the low end of his or hers.

If you find yourself straining to fill the room with sound, tuck your chin to your chest and speak in a pitch that is lower than you normally use. This will feel uncomfortable, especially for American women, many of whom are socialized to speak in a high, soft, and diminutive voice. For some women speakers, grounding the voice can feel as though they are "speaking like a man." That's exactly how it should feel. Rest assured that it only feels awkward to you because it is a lower pitch than the speaking voice you have used for years, if not decades. Work to tap into that grounded voice in presentations and in everyday conversations until it becomes second nature.

Speakers should also avoid the mistake of raising their pitch at the end of statements. Intonation rises in the last syllable or syllables of a question in Standard American English. But some speakers, most often young speakers and women, engage in "upspeak" or high rising intonation (HRI) at the end of declarative sentences. This vocal pattern undermines credibility because it suggests that the speaker is questioning his or her own statements and can be associated with a "Valley Girl" speaking pattern.

Beyond aiding projection and avoiding HRI, deep voices are often associated with credibility and leadership ability. In fact, lower voices have been correlated empirically with higher salaries among executives [1] and higher favorability ratings among political candidates.[2] While you can't change your voice to sound like Dennis Haysbert, the spokesman for Allstate Insurance, you certainly can train yourself to speak at the low end of your natural range to reap the benefits of a lower-pitched voice.

RATE

Next, work on speaking slowly and clearly. When presenters get nervous, and most public speakers do, they tend to talk at a fast clip. Andrew Dlugan did an analysis of nine popular talks on the TED website, which is a platform for viewing recordings of thought-provoking presentations given at TED conferences by subject experts and thought leaders. He found that the average rate of these speakers was 163 words per minute.[3]

You can compare your rate of speech by watching a recording of your presentation and counting the number of words you say during the course of one minute. Keep in mind that the faster you go, the harder it is for listeners to keep up with our thoughts, and the easier it is for you to use junk words (such as "um," "ah," "like," and "so").

Remember to speak more slowly than you think you should. You can do this by crisply articulating every sound, which makes it nearly impossible to rush.

And pause between sentences, which prevents thoughts from running into each other and speeches from getting faster and faster as they progress.

TONE

Speaking loudly, lowly, slowly, and clearly is a good start, but not the entire story when it comes to using your voice to its full potential. Just think of the iconic example of Ben Stein playing the boring economics teacher in the 80's film *Ferris Bueller's Day Off.* His painfully monotone voice would call out, "Bueller . . . Bueller . . ." when he was taking roll.

When presenting, take care to vary your tone by emphasizing certain words and inflecting your voice to infuse your words with those "shades of deeper meaning." Take for example the statement:

<u>Jane</u> didn't <u>drive</u> <u>her</u> <u>car</u> into the <u>house</u>.

If you read this sentence five times, each time emphasizing a different underlined portion, you can radically alter the meaning of the sentence. For instance, to emphasize Jane in this sentence suggests that someone other than Jane drove her car into the house.

SPEAKING SPEED BUMPS
Do you talk too fast? Use these "speaking speed bumps" to slow down

Raleen Miller, an accent modification specialist and speech language pathologist in Washington, D.C., articulated four "speaking speed bumps" to help her non-native English speaking clients slow down their speaking rate and improve their intelligibility to listeners. But regardless of your native tongue, they are great strategies for any presenter who tends to speak at a fast clip.

1. Drop Your Jaw (DYJ)

Open your mouth wider and move your jaw/chin downward.

- Do this for words containing: short "a," as in: at, Adam, band, banana, value, fan, fast, gas, man, snap, capital, panda, package, pants, and;
- Do this for words containing: short "o," as in: October, lock, stock, rock, Robert, rocket, dominoes, dock, taco, oxygen, cot, lot;
- Do this for words containing the "aw" sound, as in: law, auto, sausage, saw, gone, August, yawn, all, always.

2. Stretch Your Vowels (SYV)

Do this for words that contain long "e" in the initial, medial, or final position. Retract your lips further back than usual and sustain the long "e" sound. That means you should smile more when saying words such as: me, he, she, either, coffee, even, eat, east, piece, neat, lead, see, seat, mean, and leader.

3. Two Lips Together (TLT)

During a speech or in daily conversation, whenever you pause, make it a habit to put your two lips together. You should actually feel your lips touching each other. This one movement will significantly diminish your speech rate. (continued on next page)

You might be wondering, "When should I pause?" Here are a few suggestions:

- After a phrase, within a lengthy sentence

- Between sentences

- Right after you greet someone, before you begin the actual conversation, such as, "Hello, Mike." (TLT) Or, "Good afternoon, Senator." (TLT)

- After responding to a question where the first word you speak is "yes" or "no," and you follow with further comment. For example, somebody at work asks you if you have voted today. You answer by saying, "No." (TLT) "I'm going to vote on my way home from work."

4. Punch Your Final Consonants (PYFC)

Emphasize the following final consonant sounds: p, b, d, t, k, g. By doing this, you will slow your rate and people will better understand the words you are speaking. Examples of some words for which you can do this include: that, but, don't, could, help, good, up, lead, lack, mood, head, speak, hired, look, world, had, called, about, hard, right, left, it, important, difficult, can't, bag, and big.

It is unlikely that you will be discussing driving cars into houses. However, you will be delivering messages to audiences and attempting to convey specific meanings. The use of the voice to highlight those meanings will make you a more effective communicator.

To make the most of your voice as a speaker and to infuse your words with meaning, focus on volume, pitch, rate, and tone. Once you master these basics, then you can turn your focus to vocal variety.

If variety is the spice of life, then vocal variety truly is the spice of speeches. For example, consider increasing your volume when you repeat a key word or phrase in your speech. The increase in volume, along with the repetition, will make the word or phrase stand out to listeners. Also use a loud whisper to get the attention of your audience. When this technique is used during storytelling, it lends drama and adds suspense to your message.

In terms of rate, you can increase your speed as you reach the climax of a story, then pause, and tell the resolution of the situation in an especially slow, controlled pace. And in terms of pitch, you can increase the range of high and low tones in your speaking. This is easiest to do when telling stories and either going into the voices of characters or recreating sounds (say, for example, the screech of your fender as it rubbed the metal pole in your parking garage). Such vocal variations can make the difference between boring your audience and infusing your words with those "shades of deeper meaning."

EXERCISE

Deliver a practice speech in a conference room or classroom with the door closed. Recruit a friend, colleague, or classmate to stand outside the door and listen to your speech. Ground and project your voice such that the person outside the room can hear you. He or she should knock on the door whenever your voice trails off and becomes difficult to hear.

Then, invite your collaborator back in the room and deliver your speech a second time, using the same vocal volume that you did the first time. After this iteration of your speech, ask your collaborator how he or she perceived your vocal quality. Was it too loud? Did it sound commanding and confident? What did you learn about your vocal volume? How will you apply what you learned to future speeches?

ACTIVITY

Listen to a program on NPR (National Public Radio), Public Radio International (PRI), or American Public Media (APM). Some good choices are *All Things Considered, Marketplace, Fresh Air, A Prairie Home Companion,* and *This American Life,* though there may be other local offerings you can consider as well.

As you listen to the program, describe the vocal qualities of the speakers, which may include the host, guests, newsmakers, reporters, or commentators. Reflect on your attitudes toward the various speakers and how your feelings may have been informed by each speaker's vocal qualities. What conclusions can you draw about vocal qualities such as volume, pitch, rate, and tone? What can you do to improve the quality of your voice and audience member's attitudes/feelings toward you in future presentations? ▪

---

1. Mayew, William J., Christopher A. Parsons, and Mohan Venkatachalam. "Voice Pitch and the Labor Market Success of Male Chief Executive Officers." *Evolution and Human Behavior* 34.4 (2013): 243-248. Print.

2. Klofstad, Casey A., Rindy C. Anderson, and Susan Peters. "Sounds like a winner: voice pitch influences perception of leadership capacity in both men and women." *Proceedings B of the Royal Society* 279.1738 (2012): 2698-2704. Print.

3. Dlugan, Andrew. "What Is the Average Speaking Rate?" *Six Minutes.* Six Minutes: 12 Nov. 2012. Web. 16 Oct. 2013.

—— CHAPTER 6 ——

HOW YOU SAY IT
Smile

It is no wonder that in our age of hectic schedules, constant contact, and instant gratification, speakers often ask: What is the fastest and easiest way to improve my presentation?

The answer is a no-brainer: Smile. That's right; show your pearly whites.

Before further explanation is offered, please don't confuse this fast and easy way to improve a presentation with a fast and easy way to become an excellent speaker. The latter requires hard work and dedication.

But when it comes to making a marked improvement in a presentation in a short amount of time, there is nothing easier a speaker can do to bolster their perceived level of confidence than remembering to smile and show enthusiasm.

After all, everyone can smile. Yet, most speakers don't because they are nervous. At times, listeners can read nervousness for what it is. Even worse, they might perceive it as discomfort, aloofness, or even disinterest.

Speakers should smile throughout their presentations. Doing so conveys confidence and gives the audience the impression that a presenter is comfortable at the lectern, even if her or she feels quite nervous. It also causes listeners to smile back and starts a positive feedback loop (the speaker is encouraged by the positive reaction from listeners, boosting his or her confidence and enthusiasm, which in turn, causes audience members to smile and give more positive feedback).

Smiling also helps build rapport with the audience because it makes the speaker appear friendly, likeable, and approachable. And the stronger the connection a speaker builds with his or her listeners, the more likely the audience will pay attention and respond favorably to his or her message.

Many speakers don't think they should smile during a technical or serious presentation. On the contrary, a dull status report is screaming for an enthusiastic, smiling presenter. Don't worry about appearing cheesy or silly. Smiling makes you come across as passionate about your topic, which is important. After all, if you don't appear to care about your message, your audience surely won't either.

Of course, at times when it really would send the wrong message to smile—announcing layoffs or other bad news—make sure you are using facial expressions that reflect your concern, disappointment, or another appropriate emotion.

Smiling throughout a presentation sounds easy enough, but can be hard to remember when nerves kick in. Here are a few crucial times to smile:

THE GOLDEN RULE OF SMILING

As listeners, it is all too easy to forget what it's like to be on the other side of the lectern. The occasional smile or affirming nod when a speaker makes eye contact can go a long way to show support and encouragement. The Golden Rule seems quite applicable here: Do unto other speakers as you would have other speaker's do unto you. The occasional smile from an audience member is something that all presenters can appreciate.

BEFORE YOU SAY A WORD

After you make your way to the lectern, get comfortable by arranging your notes, adjusting the microphone, and taking a sip of water. Then, look up from your notes and smile. Hold that smile for a few seconds as you look out at your audience. Take a deep breath and then say the first word of your speech.

Starting with a smile will set the tone of your presentation and increase the chances you'll smile throughout the entire speech.

WHEN YOU ARE STRUGGLING

Whether you are struggling with advancing your PowerPoint slides or finding your place in your notes, smile when things aren't going as planned in your speech. Most speakers will give cues, visual (like grimacing) or auditory (like a prolonged "ummmmm"), which show they are frustrated. Rather than pointing out to your audience that there is a hiccup in your presentation, put on a genuine smile (not a sheepish one), stay silent, and continue when you're ready. By smiling during these uncomfortable moments in your speech, your audience might not even notice you were thrown off.

AT THE END OF YOUR SPEECH

You just said the last word of your presentation. Now, it's time to look out at your audience and smile. Take in the applause; you earned this moment.

Rushing off the stage is a sign that you aren't confident. Stand still for a moment before gathering your materials, leaving the lectern, and shaking hands with the emcee or person who will follow you on the agenda.

Smiling before you start speaking, when you have a hiccup in your speech, and while your audience is clapping at the conclusion of your speech certainly will help you get in the habit of flashing your pearly whites. But work toward smiling throughout your presentation too.

You can remind yourself to smile by writing the word "smile" on your outline or by drawing a smiley face on a sticky note and affixing it somewhere on the lectern where only you can see it. Every time you glance down, you will remember to smile.

Another way to remind yourself to smile is to put a small memento on the lectern that will catch your eye whenever you see it. Select something that immediately puts a smile on your face—a small gift from a family member, a trinket from a special trip, or a homemade craft from a child in your life. Lastly, you might identify something in the room where you are speaking that will remind you to smile as you're looking out at your audience. Cheerful decorations, such as flowers or balloons, are excellent choices.

COMMIT YOURSELF TO SMILING WHEN YOU SPEAK, EVEN IF YOU ARE FEELING NERVOUS. SOON ENOUGH, YOU WILL FEEL AS CONFIDENT ON THE INSIDE AS YOU LOOK ON THE OUTSIDE.

The simple act of smiling may be the fastest way to make the biggest improvement in a speech. But, it takes time to get into the habit of smiling throughout a presentation. Commit yourself to smiling when you speak, even if you are feeling nervous. Soon enough, you will feel as confident on the inside as you look on the outside when you're wearing a smile.

EXERCISE

You might not think to practice smiling; it seems somewhat vain to do so. But knowing what you look like when you speak can be very informative. Record and review a presentation on your phone, tablet, or laptop with no sound. How often did you smile? At what points in the speech did you remember to smile? When could you have smiled more? How enthusiastic do you think your listeners would rate you? How did the level of enthusiasm you observe on video compare with the level of enthusiasm you thought you conveyed while you delivered it? What can you do to show more enthusiasm in future presentations?

ACTIVITY

Smiling is important for audience members too. The next time you find yourself in a small group setting where a presentation is occurring, consciously engage the speaker through your facial expressions. It is important not to overdo it (you don't want the speaker to be alarmed by a sudden change in expression). When you smiled, how did the speaker's eye contact, tone, pitch, volume, or body language change? Based on this activity, what will you do differently in the future as an audience member and as a speaker? ▪

—————— CHAPTER 7 ——————

HOW YOU SAY IT
Silence

Perhaps your middle-school algebra teacher also said repeatedly: "Silence is golden, so let's get rich." This saying may not have been overly effective in getting adolescents to pay attention in math class, but this saw is excellent advice for presenters. Silence is a powerful tool for speakers—both in terms of avoiding filler words and adding dramatic pauses.

Whether presenting a formal speech or engaging in a workplace conversation, avoid using "junk" words—filler words and phrases that don't add meaning to your message. Some common junk words are "um," "uh," "like," "so," and "you know." But speakers can use almost any word, phrase, or sound, such as "specifically," "precisely," "now," "ladies and gentlemen," and even lip smacking, as a verbal crutch. So-called inarticulates have become commonplace in conversational Standard American English, even with political elites and corporate leaders.

Extemporaneous and impromptu speakers often use these verbal crutches to buy time when they are transitioning from one idea to the next because they aren't relying on a script. The use of such words make speakers appear less polished and can distract listeners. When used to excess, junk words can even undermine a speaker's credibility.

A case in point is Caroline Kennedy. In late 2008, she sought an appointment to fill the Senate seat that soon would be vacated by Hillary Clinton, who then was awaiting confirmation to run the U.S. State Department.

In media interviews about serving as the junior senator from New York, Kennedy littered her remarks with junk works, especially "you know" and "um." Here is just one sentence from a media interview that illustrates the problem: "You know, I think, really, um, this is sort of a unique moment, both in our, you know, in our country's history and in, you know, my own life, and, um, you know, we are facing, you know, unbelievable challenges." Kennedy, who earned an undergraduate degree from Radcliffe College and law degree from Columbia Law School, managed to sound like a ditz.

Soon, Kennedy's use of junk words became the focus of media attention. For example, there was an infamous New York Times interview transcript published on December 27, 2008, where Kennedy uses "you know" 138 times. Soon, videos popped up on YouTube that counted the number of junk words she used.

Less than a month after floating her candidacy, Kennedy abruptly withdrew her name from consideration for appointment to the Senate seat. Her use of junk words likely wasn't the sole reason for her change of heart, but it could not have helped. It seemed that many wrote off her candidacy because she was inarticulate—she was, in essence, disqualified before making a case about her qualifications and platform.

Kennedy's short-lived bid for the U.S. Senate is an important cautionary tale about excising junk words from your speaking—whether you're using the extemporaneous mode to present, speaking off the cuff to answer a question, or just having a conversation. You don't want listeners to discount the content of your message because it is delivered with a strong dose of junk words.

How, then do you trash the junk words? Speakers first must make peace with silence. Americans generally are uncomfortable with silence. At the lectern, that manifests in the tendency to speak quickly, to punctuate thoughts with junk words, and to turn sentences into run-ons by connecting them with "and."

But silence is an important part of speaking. There should be a pause between ideas and sentences to provide clarity for listeners and to give them a moment to process what they just heard.

THERE SHOULD BE A PAUSE BETWEEN IDEAS AND SENTENCES TO PROVIDE CLARITY FOR LISTENERS AND TO GIVE THEM A MOMENT TO PROCESS WHAT THEY JUST HEARD.

Speakers also tend to use junk words when they lose their train of thought. Even if listeners know you're struggling with your next thought, it is better to show poise by staying silent, rather than to fill in the time with junk words or other cues that reveal your frustration. Rest assured that a five-second pause to refer to your notes or to gather your thoughts may feel uncomfortable to you, but is inconsequential to audience members.

If silence feels awkward to most speakers, how can you get comfortable with pausing rather than using junk words?

IDENTIFY JUNK WORDS AND WHEN YOU USE THEM

The first step toward eliminating junk words is becoming aware of which ones you use and when you use them. To get started, carefully watch a recording of a past presentation and document when you use junk words and which junk words you tend to use. Soon, you will become aware of your use of junk words. When you can hear them yourself in real time, focus on excising them from your speaking in formal and informal situations alike. After all, if you can't avoid junk words in a causal conversation at the water cooler, it isn't likely you will avoid them during a high-stakes client pitch or job interview.

SLOW YOUR RATE

A major factor that contributes to the use of junk words is speaking too fast. When speakers get nervous, their hearts pound and they are off to the races with their speaking pace. That, coupled with our fear of silence, often leads to the use of junk words. To slow your rate, exaggerate the movements of your face and mouth to articulate sounds and words clearly and carefully. In addition to helping eliminate junk words, slowing your rate and adding pauses between sentences will give your audience a moment to catch up with what you're saying and file it away mentally—something for which they will be grateful.

STUDY COMEDY

A good friend once said that "we can learn a lot about the eloquence of silence" by watching the greats of comedy. He's absolutely right. He pointed out Jack Benny's ability to stand on stage in silence waiting for laughter to build. And then there's Bill Cosby, who gets laughs from the facial expressions and gestures he makes during the silence between sentences.

Replacing junk words with silence is necessary for speakers to sound crisp and confident. After you get comfortable with silence, work to use it strategically to add meaning and drama to a presentation.

Consider adding a long pause after you hit on a key point. Then, repeat the point. It is what professors do when they are covering materials that will be on an exam. Listeners know that when you say something slowly, pause, and repeat the point, they should pay close attention. You can also employ silence when telling stories. Pause before the resolution of conflict to build suspense and add drama.

Silence truly is golden and speakers should aim to get rich. Seventh grade math teacher Mr. Jostes would be glad to know that lessons from his math instruction have endured.

EXERCISE

Enlist the help of a friend, colleague, or classmate who is a good listener to alert you of your use of junk words. During a practice speech, your helper can raise a hand or a piece of paper every time he or she hears you use a junk word. If you're more of an auditory learner, it might help to have your helper drop a coin in a glass jar or click a retractable pen every time you use a junk word.

Next, practice your presentation again. This time, have your listener yell out, "Pause, one, two, three" at the end of each sentence. It drowns out whatever you start to say and soon will train you to take a purposeful pause at the end of each sentence. During this silence, formulate how you will start the next sentence and avoid leading with a junk word (especially "so").

ACTIVITY

Watch a recording of your favorite comedian. Observe how he or she uses silence. How long are the pauses? How does silence foster humor? How does it convey confidence? What principles from the comedian's use of silence can you apply to pauses in your own speaking (humorous or not)? ▪

―――― ― CHAPTER 8 ― ――――

HOW YOU SAY IT
Sight

We all have heard the adage, "The eyes are the window to the soul." They also are a ticket to a well-received presentation. After all, making eye contact with members of your audience is key to conveying confidence and establishing rapport.

LOOK UP FROM YOUR MATERIALS

Think back to a speech when the presenter was reading a script with his or her nose buried in the text. It can be painful. Presenting from a manuscript is difficult to do well; it not only requires expertly written material to achieve a conversational tone, but it also requires copious rehearsal and ideally a TelePrompTer to simulate eye contact with audience members.

Because most speakers aren't trained speechwriters, don't have the time to commit to practice reading a script until it reads naturally, and don't have a TelePrompTer, they generally should use the extemporaneous mode—speaking from a well-researched and rehearsed outline—so they can look at people in their audience and talk to them, rather than read to them.

For the majority of speakers, then, the first step toward making great eye contact is using an outline consisting of words and phrases, rather than reading a word-for-word script or PowerPoint slides filled with text. This forces presenters to speak conversationally and frees their eyes to look up from notes.

MAKE LASTING EYE CONTACT

After the eyes are freed to look up, speakers then must make lasting eye contact. Scanning the room without maintaining direct eye contact with any audience member won't cut it. Also, avoid focusing on something other than the audience (e.g., glancing out a window, up at the ceiling, or down at the floor).

Don't even think of focusing your gaze on the wall in the back of the room—above the heads of your listeners. This behavior will seem strange to audience members—they might actually look behind them to see what it is that you are looking at.

Instead, look directly at someone in the audience while saying a sentence or making one complete point—three full seconds of unbroken eye contact is ideal. (Note that unbroken eye contact means no blinking or glances up or down.) Rest assured that three seconds of unbroken eye contact is not a stare down; it is a sign of a confident speaker who is connecting with listeners.

Lasting eye contact might feel awkward to some presenters, particularly ones who aren't in the habit of making lasting eye contact in everyday conversations. Such speakers can practice by increasing the amount of time they lock their gaze with listeners in informal speaking situations. This will lay the groundwork for making excellent eye contact with audience members in formal presentations.

COORDINATE BODY POSITION WITH GAZE

Once you are making lasting eye contact, increase your connection with listeners by turning your head and body to face the person you're looking at (as opposed to keeping your head and body positioned straight ahead and looking out of the corner of your eye). Also, remember to keep your chin down; nobody in your audience wants you to look down your nose at them. Then, repeat this sustained, quality eye contact with another person in the audience in another part of the room.

Aim to make lasting eye contact with as many audience members as you can. For big audiences, make lasting eye contact with a random selection of people in different parts of the room. Though it would be impossible to lock eyes with every listener, you can give the illusion that you are. That's because listeners behind the audience member who you lock eyes with will think you are making direct eye contact with them too.

AIM TO MAKE LASTING EYE CONTACT WITH AS MANY AUDIENCE MEMBERS AS YOU CAN. FOR BIG AUDIENCES, MAKE LASTING EYE CONTACT WITH A RANDOM SELECTION OF PEOPLE.

Because the eyes truly are the window to the soul, making lasting eye contact is crucial for demonstrating your confidence as a presenter as well as establishing a connection with listeners. Effectively maintaining your gaze with audience members requires practice—practice getting comfortable holding eye contact and with the content of a presentation so you don't have to refer to notes constantly.

EXERCISE

In a group environment, have each audience member raise his or her hand. Have a speaker recite the Pledge of Allegiance (or another memorized passage) as if it was a presentation. When the speaker makes three seconds of sustained eye contact with an audience member, that listener should put his or her hand down. In a group of 15 or fewer people, have the speaker repeat the Pledge until he or she makes sustained eye contact with each audience member. In a larger setting, have the speaker say the Pledge two or three times, working to connect in a meaningful way with multiple (but not all) members of the audience who are sitting in different parts of the room.

ACTIVITY

Enlist the help of a friend, colleague, or classmate. Make sustained eye contact with your partner for three full seconds by counting aloud, "One Mississippi, two Mississippi, three Mississippi." How did it feel to engage in eye contact for this length of time? Did you have the impulse to blink or glance away? What can you do to more effectively maintain eye contact with people you are speaking to? ▪

———— CHAPTER 9 ————

HOW YOU SAY IT
Modes of Speaking

Selecting the appropriate method for delivering a presentation has a big impact on both the process (whether you make good use of time) and product (whether you give a strong presentation). What follows is an overview of the four methods of speech delivery—two scripted, two unscripted—and when to use them:

MANUSCRIPT

The manuscript mode of speaking entails thoroughly researching a presentation, writing it word-for-word, and rehearsing its recitation. It makes sense in situations when exactness of message is imperative, such as a president's State of the Union Address. For students and professionals, however, the manuscript mode is problematic because the process of scripting a speech is time consuming, the resulting presentation doesn't sound engaging because most speakers aren't trained to write for the ear, it is difficult to make eye contact while reading, and the comfort of having a text often leads to little or no practice. Most speakers should limit the use of the manuscript mode to short presentations, such as a speech of introduction.

MEMORIZED

The memorized mode of speaking requires researching a presentation, scripting it word-for-word, committing it to memory, and practicing its recitation.

Best for short presentations like toasts and acceptance speeches, which come across as more sincere when the speaker does not rely on a script or notes, the memorized mode is the most time intensive method of preparation. Beyond the problems of being time consuming as well as sounding like an essay rather than a speech, there also is the real risk of completely blanking out in front of an audience. Unlike a play you were in during elementary school, however, your teacher will not be waiting in the wings to bail you out by whispering your lines.

IMPROMPTU

The impromptu mode of speaking is markedly different in that the speaker does not have time to research and rehearse; it is off-the-cuff speaking. Situations that call for impromptu speaking include job interviews, media interviews, and question and answer sessions. Despite what the term "impromptu" implies, a speaker should practice for these moments. In most cases, the speaker can anticipate and rehearse expected questions or topics. But in the actual speaking situation, he or she only has a few moments to gather thoughts before responding. Impromptu speaking is conducive for a conversational speaking tone, but it also can lead to presentations that are unclear in purpose or that include distracting tangents. Speakers should never use the impromptu mode of speaking as a substitute for adequately researching and rehearsing a speech. It is not a method of delivery that is selected so much as it is demanded of a speaker by virtue of the occasion.

EXTEMPORANEOUS

The extemporaneous mode of speaking blends the conversational style of impromptu speaking with the thorough preparation associated with the manuscript and memorized methods of delivery. Speakers using this mode of speaking must thoroughly research their topic, craft a detailed outline (as opposed to a word-for-word script), and rehearse speech delivery. Extemporaneous speaking is especially useful for presentations that are more than a few minutes long and for speakers who don't have the luxury of a speechwriter—which means it is the mode of speaking that should be used most of the time by most speakers. Most importantly, the extemporaneous mode supports dynamic speech delivery. Here are four reasons why:

MOST IMPORTANTLY, THE EXTEMPORANEOUS MODE SUPPORTS DYNAMIC SPEECH DELIVERY.

1. MORE TIME TO REHEARSE

Because extemporaneous speaking requires a researched outline rather than a script, speakers can focus more on rehearsing the speech than on writing it. Unsurprisingly, the more you practice, the smoother your delivery. And with the focus on speaking conversationally, presenters can pay more attention to elements of dynamic delivery than mastering the exact wording of a text.

2. MORE CONVERSATIONAL

Because an extemporaneous speech isn't scripted, you avoid the problem of writing for the eye and not the ear. That is to say that most people are trained to write for readers rather than listeners. This leads to the use of words, phrases, and conventions that don't translate well to the spoken word. For example, speakers routinely use contractions and incomplete sentences, but most writers do not. By using a detailed outline as a guide, an extemporaneous speaker sees a word or phrase that prompts discussion of a particular point. Each time that point is explained, it will be a little different, but it will always be in the speaker's conversational voice.

3. MORE FLEXIBLE

If listeners look confused after hearing an argument, an extemporaneous speaker can easily provide another example or further explanation and then move seamlessly to the next argument. But delivering a speech using the manuscript or memorized methods of delivery greatly reduces the responsiveness of a speaker to his or her audience. For example, when a speaker is reading a manuscript, he or she might not be looking up from the script enough to detect audience confusion in the first place, let alone deviate from the prepared text and smoothly transition back to it. And in terms of the memorized method of delivery, any deviation from the text can make it difficult to get back on track because most people remember information in the order it was committed to memory. Change things up during your memorized presentation and you run the risk of forgetting the rest of your lines.

4. FEWER FREEZES

For many speakers, the most convincing benefit of extemporaneous speaking, and a reason in and of itself to use this mode of speaking whenever possible, is the ability to get back on track with your speech when you "freeze." We've all been there—up in front of an audience with no idea what to say next.

For a manuscript speech, you can freeze if you go off script or lose your place when looking up from the text. An even more disruptive freeze can happen if your text gets out of order or is missing a page. For a memorized speech, a catastrophic freeze can occur if you forget your line and don't have a script to refer to. And for an impromptu speech, it's all too easy to freeze because you don't have time to organize your thoughts before speaking.

HOW TO IMPROVE DELIVERY OF A MANUSCRIPT SPEECH

Formatting to Find your Place

- Print it big (at least 14 pt font)
- Page break at main points—and avoid page break mid paragraph
- Add an extra blank line between sections
- Consider formatting key topic sentence in bold or adding section headings

Marking for Delivery

Underline sell sentences (The 5-10 most important lines, often summing up a point.)

- "|" one horizontal line for a short pause, 2 or 3 lines to indicate a longer pause.
- "/" a slash at contrast points and words such as "however" or "yet"
- "()" parenthetical marks indicate asides
- In the margins, put comments about delivery and stage directions. An arrow alongside a paragraph may remind you to build its intensity. Write the word "slow" next to section where you will slow down to teach or to sell. Write other words (such as "pensive" or "angry") that describe the tone the delivery will adopt to pull out the subtext. Add stage directions that will remind you to walk to the center of the room, point to a picture on the wall, etc.

Practicing With the Script

- Examine the structure first. Plan to learn the speech section by section.
- Memorize cold the start of intro and the concluding lines.

HOW TO IMPROVE DELIVERY OF A MANUSCRIPT SPEECH
(continued)

- Practice each section out loud. Ideally, learn each section so that you could deliver it without the script. The goal is not to recite the script precisely word for word, but to hold it "in res"—certainly more closely memorized than an extemporaneous speech delivered from an outline.

- As you practice out loud, trying to get away from script, keep a pen in your hand so that you can return to the script and revise it! You will hear yourself say things that aren't in the script that sound better than the script. You will read things in the script that don't sound very good out loud. Fix them. This is writing for the ear.

- Remember to practice from the script that you will use when you present! Minor adjustments aside, you should not create new page breaks, increase the font, add a heading, etc. after you have practiced. Our minds work spatially. If you make a dramatic change to where the content appears on a page, then you might not be able to easily locate a passage if you get stuck. At that point, the usefulness of the manuscript is greatly decreased.

- Do ensure that sell lines are memorized so that on those lines you can give full eye contact.

- After the speaking engagement, return to the script to make changes.

Even the most seasoned speakers freeze. What's important is your ability to get back on track. The surest way to recover quickly is using the extemporaneous method of delivery. When you lose your place and don't know what to say next, just look at your outline, pause while you find the word or phrase to remind you of your next point, look back up at the audience, smile, and continue with your presentation. So long as you don't show outward signs of panic or frustration, your audience likely won't know there was a hiccup in your speech.

There are some times when it makes sense to use a manuscript or memorized mode of speaking, or when a presenter is in a situation that demands an impromptu response. But whenever it is appropriate to use notes, which is the case in most professional and academic speaking situations, opt for the extemporaneous mode of speaking. Not only will you save time and make your delivery more dynamic, you can also take much of the fear out of presenting by giving yourself the security of an outline that prevents catastrophic freezes.

EXERCISE

Write down five questions on notecards or scraps of paper. These should be questions that are relevant to an upcoming presentation, questions that you are often asked, or questions on subjects that you know well. Have a friend, colleague, or classmate ask you the questions and record your responses. Then, answer each question again, but present your response as if you were delivering a memorized speech on that subject. Review the videos of your responses. How did your delivery change from the first to the second take for each question? How can this exercise inform your future off-the-cuff responses to questions or impromptu presentations?

ACTIVITY

List the types of speaking situations that you find yourself engaging in on a weekly or monthly basis (such as meetings, keynote addresses, client pitches, informational briefings, panel presentations, speeches of introduction, etc.). What mode of speaking do you usually use in each of the speaking situation you listed? How would changing the mode of speaking affect your preparation, tone, recall of specific information, flexibility to adapt to cues from listeners, ability to make lasting eye contact, and ability to meet the goals of the presentation? ∎

—— CHAPTER 10 ——

WHAT YOU SAY
Ethics

In a college classroom, a student who asserts a fact in a speech or paper without citing the source can be accused of academic dishonesty (or at the very least, sloppy work). But in U.S. politics, the president can deliver a 45-minute speech, full of facts, without a single attribution to a source. Is the latter unethical? Or are universities overly sensitive to issues of plagiarism?

Perhaps even trickier is the following situation: You are tasked with giving a sales report. You are fairly certain that you are the only person who will look closely at the numbers. Do you round up the numbers to create a better depiction of the sales? After all, it is just rounding up numbers? It'll be easier for audience members to comprehend and remember round numbers, right?

These scenarios represent the difficulty of talking about ethics in presenting. Ethics, like so much of public speaking, is about the relationship between a speaker, the message, and the audience. What might seem unethical in one set of circumstances would not raise an eyebrow in another.

The guiding principle to speaking ethically is to respect vigilantly the three elements of the presentation: treat your message, your audience, and yourself with respect, and do so with a heightened sense of awareness.

VIGILANTLY RESPECT YOUR MESSAGE

Respecting the message involves doing many things that the audience will never hear or see. These include verifying supporting material that you found in a second-hand account, checking the veracity of claims made by others that you intend to use in your presentation, avoiding the use of statistics that may be helpful to your argument but that are inconsistent with the bulk of research on the topic, and making sure that facts are not taken out of context.

And of course, ethical speakers don't plagiarize—intentionally or unintentionally using another person's words or ideas without attribution. There is broad consensus that speakers shouldn't pass off the material of others as their own. But the fuzzier question comes when we ask what material speakers should cite in their speeches and how.

Though the president may not cite material in speeches, journalists and fact-checking websites make it their job to verify the facts presented. For most speakers, however, presentations are not scrutinized to this degree. That's why it is helpful to provide thorough oral citations and even useful descriptions about the authors and publications cited. Such due diligence serves to boost your credibility (even if it hasn't been the norm at your organization or in a particular situation).

If you are unfamiliar with the expectations of your audience, err on the side of caution and give credit to your sources orally. Just like the rule of thumb for dressing for a presentation—you'd rather do too much than too little.

To cite a source in your presentation, include the name of the author, the publication, and the publication date. It is a good idea to provide introductory phrases that give listeners context about the author's credentials, the publication's pedigree, and the type of publication if such information likely would be unfamiliar to an informed audience member.

Here is an example: "In his *New York Times* bestselling book *The Tipping Point*, published in 2000, journalist and staff writer at *The New Yorker* Malcom Gladwell sought to explain how ideas and messages 'spread like viruses do.' "

This may seem like a lot of information to say aloud. It is—and for good reason. Audience members don't have the luxury of flipping through a printed works cited or bibliography if they want to find a source you mention in your speech. As such, you need to provide enough information orally, at the time you introduce specific information in a speech, for listeners to find the source material on their own, without an undue amount of searching.

VIGILANTLY RESPECT YOUR AUDIENCE

Respecting your audience begins with topic selection. For starters, remember that presentations are about your audience and not you. Don't frame your subject in terms of what you want to talk about; frame it in terms of the value you can provide the audience based on their needs and interests. In other words, make it about them (the audience), not you (the speaker). (See chapter 13 for more on topic selection.)

On the other hand, make sure that you are identifying with audience members and not pandering to them. Manipulating speech elements in a way that compromises the integrity of the message for the sole purpose of currying the favor of the audience fails to respect the message, audience, and speaker.

Also, you should never be dishonest about your intentions for speaking. Presenters who are selling products and services can get in trouble when they "sell from the lectern." Listeners often feel duped when this occurs. On the other hand, providing valuable information to listeners during your presentation without pushing products can start building trust and goodwill with audience members who then become more apt to purchase your goods or services in the long run.

When you do land on a topic that is consistent with your beliefs and helpful to listeners, work to tailor your examples, stories, and suggestions to them. If you are a nutrition expert speaking to college students, provide examples of nutrition content of food and drinks from popular campus restaurants (rather than high-end national chains that students can't afford and don't frequent); benefits that diet changes have reaped for young adults (rather than middle-aged people); and, advice on eateries on or near campus that offer healthful options (rather than focusing on how to cook meals in a full kitchen).

As you tailor your message to your audience, be mindful that you don't stereotype audience members or talk down to them. For example, you may offend listeners by assuming that all college students binge drink or by dumbing down your description of a metabolic process. (See chapter 12 for more on analyzing situations and audiences).

AS YOU TAILOR YOUR MESSAGE TO YOUR AUDIENCE, BE MINDFUL THAT YOU DON'T STEREOTYPE AUDIENCE MEMBERS OR TALK DOWN TO THEM.

When trying to determine how much detail to include, use the "Mother-in-Law Test." Dr. Mari Boor Tonn, a rhetoric professor, said that she would have her mother-in-law read drafts of her academic papers to see if the arguments and explanations were clear and persuasive. Her mother-in-law was educated, informed, and reasonable, but not a scholar in the same academic field. Consider adopting Tonn's "Mother-in-Law Test." It is a helpful way to gauge the type of material to include in professional presentations so that you don't get too technical or offend the intelligence of your audience.

After you craft your message and supporting material, allot enough time to rehearse. Aim to practice a presentation at least six times before delivering it, as this is the point at which most speakers will become more fluent with content

USE LANGUAGE ETHICALLY

Maintaining high ethical standards extends even to the words a speaker uses.

Work to avoid language that denigrates or is hurtful to minority groups, such as women, members of the LGBT community, or people with intellectual disabilities.

Avoid gender stereotyping by using pronouns and terms that are gender inclusive. For example:

"A surgeon works long hours; he or she should expect to log at least 80 hours a week during residency." (Note: their is not a grammatically correct substitution for he or she. However, know your audience. Some groups—particularly the transgender community—use "their" to avoid gender pronouns.)

Avoid gender specific. Instead use gender neutral.

Gender Specific	Gender Neutral
Fireman	Firefighter
Stewardess	Flight attendant
Workman	Worker
Forefathers	Forbears
You guys	You all

Avoid equating homosexuality and intellectual disability with something that is undesirable or bad. For example:

Avoid insensitive
"That movie was gay."
Use instead
"That movie was terrible."

Avoid insensitive
"That's a retarded idea."
Use instead
"That's a bad idea."

and can present with a more dynamic delivery style. (See chapter 22 for more on rehearsal.)

During rehearsals, use a stopwatch to check if your presentation meets time constraints. You don't want to insult listeners and event organizers by taking more time than you have been allotted. Remember, most speakers prepare more material than they have time to deliver. Opt to pare down content and practice concise ways of making points; never speak faster to fit it all in time limits.

Delivering an under-prepared or under-rehearsed presentation reflects poorly on the speaker and is disrespectful to listeners. Don't waste the time of audience members by giving a half-baked speech.

You can also show respect to audience members after a presentation by seeking feedback. When appropriate, use questionnaires to solicit responses from listeners. In cases where this would be inappropriate or unfeasible, ask key listeners (such as a supervisor or event organizer) for their suggestions on how you can make improvements. Then, analyze the feedback and take steps to incorporate the good advice into future presentations.

VIGILANTLY RESPECT YOURSELF

As much as a speaker might know deep down that they are a good, ethical person, audience members generally can only gauge ethics of a speaker through his or her presentation. This does not mean that a speaker must elaborate extensively to get across that they are an ethical person. Rather, the character of the speaker is created by the care taken in the composition and delivery of his or her message. To take a shortcut or become sloppy in preparing and presenting can hurt a speaker's credibility. It is difficult to earn an audience's trust back; better not to lose it in the first place.

A good example of ethical presenting can be seen in a speech given by former U.S. Sen. Edward Kennedy in 1983. Kennedy, a Massachusetts Democrat and practicing Catholic, was invited to speak at the staunchly conservative Liberty Baptist College in Lynchburg, Virginia. Kennedy did not agree with many of the political positions of then-Chancellor Jerry Falwell.

It would have been unethical for liberal Kennedy to pander to the conservative audience when his own beliefs differed. However, he showed respect for the audience, made light of the incongruities of the situation with humor directed at both himself and Falwell, and managed to give a speech consistent with his views on tolerance and the state of political affairs in Washington, D.C. Judging by the reaction from the audience, listeners seemed to appreciate his honesty and efforts despite the likely difference in opinions.

Kennedy's example shows how a speaker can respect the identity of the audience without pandering, find a way to identify with even the staunchest of critics, and maintain his or her character and credibility when faced with an oppositional audience. As is the case with most questions of ethical public speaking, there isn't a clear-cut formula to "get it right." But it did take a heightened sense of awareness, thorough preparation, and a dose of courage for Kennedy to pull the feat off—exactly what speakers need to do to present ethically by vigilantly respecting their message, their audience, and themselves. ∎

—————— CHAPTER 11 ——————

WHAT YOU SAY
Outlining Speeches and the Sandwich Structure

"My typical method of preparing for a presentation included trying to memorize what I planned to say, word for word," admitted Claire Wilson, a mother of two and the executive director of research and evaluation at Insight Policy Research, a Washington, D.C.-based firm that conducts empirical research for organizations that draft public policy and advocate for its enactment. "Needless to say, this method did not serve me very well."

Like many presenters, Claire struggled with formatting her speaking material in an effective way. She spent way too much time writing and committing to memory content that was better suited for the printed page.

Other speakers have the opposite problem: they can't get started. They have ideas, but get overwhelmed looking at a blank piece of paper or an empty set of presentation slides on their computer screen. So they procrastinate, and end up with a hastily prepared speech and little rehearsal, or recycled remarks that don't fit the speaking situation.

These problems both lead to the same result: speeches that are a disappointment to both the audience and speaker. But it doesn't have to be this way.

Over years of working with clients and students, we have developed a method of outlining speeches called the Sandwich Structure. It's a unique approach that you won't find in other textbooks. Speakers swear by it because it is useful for crafting any speech, and particularly conducive to the extemporaneous mode of speaking, which we recommend professionals and students use for most speaking situations (see chapter 9 for details). The Sandwich Structure also offers a straightforward structure that works for a wide range of speeches and a step-by-step process that prevents writers block. Additionally, it encourages clear and memorable content, incorporates best practices of public speaking, and just as importantly, saves time.

Here's how it works: The Sandwich Structure rejects scripts written word for word that generally lead to a wooden and impersonal delivery style. Then, it embraces and adapts the Roman Numeral Outline you may have learned in school to sketch out papers. It makes four important changes to the Roman Numeral Outline format to better adapt to the demands and the best practices of public speaking. Here are four ways the Sandwich Structure differs from a Roman Numeral Outline:

1. It limits the outline to one page;

2. It is oriented horizontally rather than vertically;

3. It has a "Sandwich," or a section of the page marked off at the top and bottom for the speech attention getter and clincher; and,

4. It includes ocular, or visual, cues to remind speakers to incorporate several best practices of public speaking.

ONE PAGE

The first way the Sandwich Structure differs from a Roman Numeral Outline is that it is always on one sheet of paper. It doesn't matter if it's a two-minute report or two-hour seminar.

By limiting notes to just one page, the Sandwich Structure prevents a scripted presentation, which saves vast amounts of preparation time. And with just one sheet of paper, speakers must limit their outline to key words and phrases.

This helps speech delivery because it promotes extemporaneous speaking—when speakers take brief glances at their well-rehearsed notes and then talk to listeners about each idea using a conversational tone and making lasting eye contact. (For more on the modes of speaking, see chapter 9.)

ORIENTED HORIZONTALLY

Next, the Sandwich Structure differs from a Roman Numeral Outline because the page orientation is horizontal rather than vertical—so main points are organized on the paper like a timeline from left to right.

This orientation is crucial for extemporaneous speaking because it allows speakers to find their next idea quickly. When you are moving from one point to the next, or worse, at those moments in a speech when you completely lose your train of thought and freeze, the Sandwich Structure helps you recover quickly because you have the security of knowing exactly where to look on the outline to find your next point.

THE SANDWICH STRUCTURE HELPS YOU RECOVER QUICKLY BECAUSE YOU HAVE THE SECURITY OF KNOWING EXACTLY WHERE TO LOOK ON THE OUTLINE TO FIND YOUR NEXT POINT.

When the outline is limited to one page and oriented horizontally, you always know that in the beginning of your speech the applicable notes are on the left-hand side. In the middle of the presentation, they're right in the middle of the page. And toward the end of your speech, you need only to glance to the right-hand side of the page to find the word or phrase you wrote down to jog your memory for that part of your presentation.

Speaking from such an outline and in the extemporaneous mode is uncomfortable for some speakers at first, as is doing anything new. But with a little practice, you will find it easy to glance down at your Sandwich Structure Outline in the correct part of the page, find the word or phrase for the next idea in your speech, look up at the audience, smile, and speak to audience members with confidence.

The horizontal orientation also can be a tremendous time saver because it allows speakers to diagnose problems with their speech content early on in the outlining process. If in an early iteration of the Sandwich Structure you notice that the first point in your speech has six sub-points, but the second has only two, it is immediately clear the presentation lacks balance. It suggests the organization should be reconsidered; perhaps the first main point should become the subject of the entire speech, or maybe the first main point could be broken into two smaller and more manageable main points. If you write out an entire script for a speech, chances are you will have spent much more time on the content before you realize you need to tweak the organization. Or, you may never develop a clear thesis and carefully structured main points to support it—something the Sandwich Structure prompts you to do early in the process of crafting presentation content.

THE SANDWICH

The third difference between the Sandwich Structure and a Roman Numeral Outline is the presence of a "Sandwich," the namesake of this method of outlining, which refers to the portion of the page at the top and bottom of the outline that is sectioned off from the speech body with horizontal lines.

The top and bottom of the Sandwich are sectioned off so you can write the first line or two and the last line or two of the speech. But why, you might ask, would the opening and closing of the presentation be written out after great pains were taken to describe the Sandwich Structure as a rejection of a scripted approach?

Because the introduction and conclusion are the most important parts of a presentation. According to the law of primacy and recency, people most vividly remember what they hear first and last. This holds true for presentations, so you better make your opening and closing count.

Don't waste the opening lines of your speech providing biographical information about yourself (that is the purpose of having someone else give a speech of introduction), repeating the title or main idea of your presentation (you will get to this after the opening lines), or thanking the person who introduced you or the event organizer (you can thank the introducer as you shake hands and acknowledge the host after your attention getter and before you get into the body of your speech). The first words out of your mouth must be interesting, catchy, and suspenseful—grabbing the attention of audience

DON'T WASTE THE OPENING LINES OF YOUR SPEECH.

members and giving them a reason to continue listening (see chapter 20 for detail on crafting attention getters). The concluding lines of your presentation are equally important. They must signal the speech is coming to a close so listeners know you have finished and they can clap (this avoids an awkward silence after your last line and means you don't have to say "thank you" at the very end of your presentation). Accomplish this by coming full circle— your clincher should refer back, in some concrete way, to your attention getter. Effective closings also offer listeners pause for thought or an actual challenge to change their beliefs or actions (again, see chapter 20 for detail on crafting conclusions).

The Sandwich element of the Sandwich Structure ensures a strong, well-planned introduction and conclusion because these sections are written out in advance and, ideally, memorized. If nerves cause a speaker to blank out on the introduction or conclusion during a presentation, the lines are in front of him or her for last-minute review, and in worst-case scenarios, available for the speaker to read to the audience word-for-word before moving to the body of the presentation and a more extemporaneous delivery style.

Having the Sandwich is crucial to effective speech delivery because having a carefully crafted introduction and conclusion, as well as the security of knowing the lines are there for reading if necessary, makes speakers feel more confident. It allows speakers to approach and leave the lectern on a high note, even if there were a few stumbles during the body of the speech.

OCULAR CUES

The last way the Sandwich Structure departs from the Roman Numeral Outline is the inclusion of ocular, or visual, reminders to include best practices of public speaking in your presentation.

One best practice that the Sandwich Structure facilitates is overtly stating the central idea. That's why there's a place below the introduction for a speaker to write a word or phrase for the central idea of the speech. Though it sounds obvious, many speakers fail to identify and state the point of their speech early on in the presentation (or ever). In the vast majority of cases, this is advisable and will improve clarity of the overall message. (If you happen to be giving a persuasive speech to an antagonistic audience, however, you would be wise to establish your credibility and provide some support for your case before revealing your specific ask.)

Additionally, the Sandwich Structure has the word "preview" on the page just below the central idea to remind the speaker to tell audience members at the beginning of the speech how it is structured. This roadmap of the presentation lets listeners know what to expect and promotes the retention of key ideas.

Continuing with the sage advice of "tell 'em what you're gonna tell 'em, tell 'em, tell 'em what you told 'em," the Sandwich Structure includes the word "review" just above the conclusion so the speaker is reminded to recap for the audience where they went on the journey of the presentation and to reinforce main points.

Finally, the T's with boxes around them signal the speaker to transition from one idea in a presentation to the next. This ensures that listeners are never left behind when a speaker moves on to a new main point. And, it serves as another way for a speaker to hammer home ideas he or she wants audience members to remember.

Having visual cues—the central idea, preview, review, and transitions—on the Sandwich Structure means speakers remember to be clear and repetitious, which are particularly crucial when a message is delivered orally rather than in writing. And by using visual cues, speakers are prompted to follow these best practices of public speaking without lots of extra text that would make it more difficult to find speech points and sub-points on a Sandwich Structure while delivering an extemporaneous presentation.

Remember to write your Sandwich Structure in large text on a full sheet of paper or a legal-sized piece that is oriented horizontally. You also can utilize an online speech-planning tool at www.spokenwithauthority.com to craft your Sandwich Structure. It provides an easy template to fill in and offers helpful reminders to keep you on track. Using large, legible font (whether handwritten or computer generated) is key. That way, you can easily read your notes when you refer to them and can readily find the next point on your Sandwich Structure when you "freeze" and can't remember to say next. The Sandwich Structure provides many speakers piece of mind of knowing exactly where to look to find whey intended to discuss next.

Like anything new, the Sandwich Structure will take a little getting used to. But with practice, it saves time on the crafting of a presentation, improves message effectiveness, and supports an extemporaneous delivery.

Give the Sandwich Structure a try. Soon you will have success at the lectern like Claire, who reported that this method of outlining "helped me better connect with the audience and deliver presentations that were more polished and compelling. My employer was thrilled with the results and my clients were very complimentary of my subsequent presentations. By helping me to articulate my points more clearly and powerfully, I not only improved my public speaking skills, but also my professional image."

EXERCISE

Craft a Sandwich Structure of a three- to four-minute speech on a hobby or interest. The topic could be anything from knitting to photography, cooking to soccer. It should be something that you know well and are passionate about.

Then, rehearse your hobby or interest speech several times using the Sandwich Structure you crafted. Then, deliver it before an audience. Did you have enough material for four minutes? Too much? How did the experience of speaking from a Sandwich Structure differ from other materials you have used to give presentations from in the past? Were you more conversational? Did you need more rehearsals than you would if you had a word-for-word script to feel comfortable with the material?

ACTIVITY

Watch a recording of Steve Jobs's Stanford University commencement address from 2005 (www.youtube.com/watch?v=UF8uR6Z6KLc).

Create a Sandwich Structure of it. What did you learn about the speech by formatting it in the Sandwich Structure? Based on your knowledge of the Sandwich Structure and best practices of crafting presentations, what are strengths of the Jobs commencement address? How could it have been better? ∎

SAMPLE SANDWICH STRUCTURE #1

I call it the Gelman study crawl. It happens on most Sundays and in the days leading up to spring break or finals: you ride the elevator up to the sixth floor of Gelman Library. Finding the study rooms all occupied and tables overflowing, you begin a desperate downward trajectory: to the fifth floor, finding it just as crowded as the sixth; then the fourth (no luck); the third (no way); and back to the entrance. Realizing the utter futility of trying to find a decent spot in crowded "Gelhell," you give up, go home, defeated.

ALTERNATIVE STUDY SPOTS*

PREVIEW

T	**I. On-campus buildings**

   A. Rome Hall

   B. Monroe Hall

   C. 1st through 4th floors
      of Phillips Hall

   D. 2nd through 5th floors
      of Duques Hall

T	**II. Nearby coffee shops**

   A. Filter Coffee

   B. Bourbon Coffee

   C. Caribou Coffee

   D. Illy Café on
      New Hampshire Ave.

T	**III. D.C. landmarks**

   A. Library of Congress

   B. National Portrait Gallery
      Kogod Courtyard

REVIEW

If you are as tired as I am of getting crowded out of Gelman Library when you need it most, you aren't without recourse. Between other GW buildings, nearby coffee shops, and D.C.'s famous landmarks, there is a menagerie of options available to you when you finally do decide that it's time to ditch the dreaded Gelman study crawl.

---

* Based on an informative speech by Jeffrey Winters, student in COMM 3171 Professional Communication at the George Washington University

SAMPLE SANDWICH STRUCTURE #2

A few weeks ago, I went to an open mic night at Busboys and Poets, a local restaurant. I was pleasantly surprised that oral performances were being interpreted into American Sign Language (ASL).

GWU SHOULD HAVE INTERPRETERS FOR CAMPUS MUSIC CONCERTS*

PREVIEW

T **I. Hearing community at GW should be more inclusive**

A. Currently no interpreters

B. Hard of hearing and deaf still want to be included socially

C. Also, still want to understand and enjoy music (QUOTATION)

T **II. GW should use ASL students to interpret at campus concerts for class credit. Why concerts?**

A. Bass is enjoyable to hard of hearing and deaf

B. Music allows students to prepare for interpreting; a good way to gain experience and learn signs

C. VIDEO of Sign Language Rap Battle

T **III. Benefits to GW**

A. Interpreters at concerts would help unite hearing and deaf communities

B. Concerts would be more enjoyable and interesting for all attendees

C. ASL students would gain valuable experience at no cost to the university

D. Program could attract more students to GW's Speech and Hearing Sciences

REVIEW

I encourage you to join me in writing a letter to the chair of the Department of Speech and Hearing Sciences. Let's urge the department to give ASL students class credit for interpreting at campus music concerts, so that GW's campus will offer the same inclusive environment that I experienced at Busboys and Poets recently.

* Based on a persuasive speech by Hannah Koch, student in COMM 1040 Public Communication at the George Washington University

—————— CHAPTER 12 ——————

WHAT YOU SAY
Analyzing the Situation and Audience

You probably learned the five W's when you were taught how to write a report in school or an article for the school newspaper. Unfortunately, most speakers forget to ask who, what, when, where, and why before crafting a presentation. Forgetting to ask these questions is a big mistake; no matter how excellent the content and delivery of a presentation may be, it will fall short if the situation and audience aren't taken into consideration first.

For example, take the case of a government official who was scheduled to present to a prominent group of business leaders. A staff member assumed it would be a formal presentation with a lectern for notes and assured the speaker that a scripted speech was appropriate. When the speaker arrived, he actually was seated in the middle of a large conference table with audience members also seated around him. Imagine his horror!

A scripted delivery would have been a disaster in this situation—it would have come across as wooden, distant, and might even suggest that the speaker didn't know his material. On the fly, the speaker used his scripted speech as a guide from which he covered key points in a conversational way. But, knowing the set up in advance would have saved time of writing out an entire presentation and would have allowed for the preparation and rehearsal of more appropriate notes.

Also consider the case of a director of a non-profit organization who was slated to keynote an industry conference. Without taking time to learn about expected attendees, she recycled a speech that she had given successfully to a general audience. But had she done research, she would have known this conference was billed for seasoned professionals in the field and that her speech wasn't a good fit for the knowledge level and interests of her audience.

When she received a summary of evaluations of her speech, she found that while many listeners enjoyed hearing her personal story, they didn't learn new information that would help them do their work more effectively. This was a missed opportunity to impact a key audience and to gain a reputation as a dynamic speaker.

Sure, it takes extra time and effort to research the situation and audience of a speech, and to craft a unique speech based on an analysis of your research. But the dividends—giving a presentation that fits the situation, resonates with your audience, and makes you proud of your remarks—far outweigh the investment.

HERE'S HOW SPEAKERS SHOULD APPLY THE FIVE W'S WHEN PREPARING TO CRAFT A SPEECH:

WHAT IS THE OCCASION FOR MY SPEECH?

Do research on the event at which you're being asked to present. Knowing the event's purpose, tone, host, history, and expected attendees will help you decide whether to accept the invitation and what approach to take if and when you present.

Also think of the occasion broadly. Using the terminology of theorist Lloyd Bitzer, consider the exigence of your speech—the urgent problem or need that demands a rhetorical response.[1]

WHY HAVE I BEEN ASKED TO SPEAK?

Ask organizers what perspective they hope you can bring to the event. If they are looking for something that you cannot or do not want to deliver, work with planners to find a topic that works for you both or respectfully decline the invitation. If you decline, you can help maintain a strong relationship with organizers by suggesting other speakers who may be a good fit.

WHEN WILL I BE SPEAKING?

Determine the time of day you'll be giving your speech and how long event organizers would like you to speak. Add extra enthusiasm for an early-morning event, be prepared for lots of distractions during a keynote at a luncheon, and add humor to an after-dinner speech. Find out the agenda for the event at which you're presenting, when your speech falls in the order of events, and what other speakers and topics will go before and after you. Make sure your remarks relate to and even refer to other speakers or topics, but don't overlap too much.

Most importantly, respect the time limits you've been given by rehearsing in advance and tracking your time as you deliver your presentation. Keep in mind that audience attention wanes significantly after about 15 to 20 minutes (that's why TED Talks, viewable at TED.com, are limited to 18 minutes). So, aim to keep remarks short and leave time for a question and answer session. Or for longer sessions, like training programs, break your material into several shorter segments that are punctuated with videos, activities, or discussion to help aid understanding and keep listeners engaged.

WHERE WILL I BE SPEAKING?

Determine the location of your presentation and how it will be set up. A scripted speech would be appropriate for a setup with a lectern, microphone, and theater-style seating for audience members, but it would be a complete flop for an intimate talk given from a seated position at a conference table to a handful of listeners who also are sitting around it. PowerPoint would be a disaster during an after-dinner speech, but likely expected from a headliner at a business conference. Humor is difficult to pull off in speeches delivered at outdoor venues, as the sound of laughter dissipates outside and makes jokes seem less effective. And at such locations, the length of your presentation must be cut significantly if the weather is inclement. It is crucial to identify details of the location of a presentation before you craft it, but don't forget to be aware of your surroundings and the comfort of audience members on the day of your presentation.

WHO WILL I BE SPEAKING TO?

Take time to get to know your audience. Don't make assumptions. Learn what type of people you're addressing in terms of their demographics: age, ethnicity, gender, religion, political affiliation, education, occupation, and income. The U.S. Census Bureau is a treasure trove of statistical information about people in the United States. Similar data is collected and published by other organizations, like universities.

Dig even deeper by talking to event organizers and getting in touch by phone with expected attendees (complete the phone-a-friend exercise at the end of this chapter). Find out what your audience already knows about your subject and their attitudes toward it. Identify what your audience members care about and what they want to learn from you. You will be amazed by the wealth of information you glean about your listeners and the material you gather that can be used in your presentation (such as personal stories as well as points of reference shared by members of your audience).

The goal here isn't to alter your speech based on stereotypes of listeners, like making your materials pink or removing references to empirical data when speaking to an audience of women. It also isn't to pander to audience members and tell them what they want to hear; changing your views based on your audience is unethical. Rather, it's about finding the intersection of what the speaker is passionate about, what the audience is interested in, and what the occasion calls for. That is the sweet spot where excellent speeches happen. (See chapters 10 and 13 for more on ethics and topic selection respectively.)

Answering the five W's in a report or news article ensures you covered all your bases. Doing the same before crafting a presentation can prevent you from making assumptions about the situation and audience that could doom a speech before a word is delivered.

EXERCISE

Don't rely on the word of an event organizer to tell you everything you need to know about your audience. Ask him or her to give you the contact information of up to a dozen people who are expected to attend your presentation. And don't just get contact information from notable audience members or group leaders; aim to talk to a range of listeners, including average folks who will be sitting in the back of the room.

1. Conduct 15-minute phone interviews with at least six provided contacts before you start crafting your presentation. Find out what each person does, where they're from, why they're attending the event at which you'll be speaking, concerns they have about your topic, and what they hope to learn from your presentation. Don't keep to a strict list of questions. Have some open-ended questions prepared to keep the conversation flowing, but listen carefully and follow the lead of the person you're interviewing.

2. Aim to collect several interesting stories and examples; incorporate them in your presentation. (Just make sure to ask permission before using specific information during your speech.) Using material gathered this way will improve the chances that your speech will resonate with audience members, and will show them that you tailored your remarks and didn't just recycle a speech.

3. On the day of your presentation, arrive early and try to connect in person with some of the audience members you talked to on the phone. That way, you will have new friends in the audience—making it more comfortable than addressing a roomful of strangers.

ACTIVITY

Using either using one of your own past presentations or a presentation given by a noteworthy speaker, change elements of the context (such as the time, location, or audience) and consider how that message would need to change to fit the new occasion.

If you cannot think of one of your own presentations, consider this: On December 16, 2012, President Obama spoke at an interfaith vigil for the victims of a school shooting in Newtown, Connecticut (www.whitehouse.gov/the-press-office/2012/12/16/remarks-president-sandy-hook-interfaith-prayer-vigil).

How did Obama connect to the audience and the occasion? What might he have done differently to adapt his message to his interests, the audience, and the occasion? ▪

1. Bitzer, Lloyd F. "The Rhetorical Situation." *Philosophy and Rhetoric* 1.1 (1968): 1-14. Print.

CHAPTER 13

WHAT YOU SAY
Topic Selection

Many presenters make the mistake of giving short shrift to topic selection. But the ultimate success of a speech requires finding just the right subject; it deserves careful consideration.

The best presentations occur at the intersection of the passion of the speaker, the desires of audience members, and the demands of the occasion. To hit the sweet spot, consider each of the following key ingredients in the recipe for successful topic selection:

THE SPEAKER

If you aren't passionate about the topic of your speech, you won't be enthusiastic in researching, developing, rehearsing, or delivering it. For students who are required to present in class and have freedom to select a topic, avoid the temptation to go with the issue dominating this week's headlines or a "stock" topic. While you might genuinely be interested in reforming a government agency, lowering the drinking age, or legalizing marijuana, you likely don't have a deeper connection to the topic. This means that you won't be particularly motivated to work on your presentation; worse yet, on the date of your presentation, presenter before you might give a speech on the same topic. Talk about a confidence buster!

Let your personal interests and experiences guide your selection of topic. They can come from classes you've taken and jobs or internships you've held. But, they also can come from hobbies, like playing an instrument or sport, or even life experiences, such as living with a chronic medical condition or commuting on a bicycle. Such topics will encourage you to tell personal stories, which no other speaker could repeat, and speak with credibility, which no other speaker will have on that topic.

For presenters who are invited to speak at a conference or other event, you will be served well by allowing your personal interests and experiences to guide your decision to accept or decline the invitation. After all, if you accept an invitation to speak on a subject you don't know about or care about, you will frustrate yourself and disappoint your listeners.

IT IS ALWAYS FLATTERING TO RECEIVE AN INVITATION TO PRESENT. BUT RESIST THE TEMPTATION TO GIVE AN IMMEDIATE "YES."

It is always flattering to receive an invitation to present. But resist the temptation to give an immediate "yes." Ask the event organizer about the desired topic of your talk. Also, do a thorough analysis of the situation and audience (see chapter 12 for details) to make sure the event organizer's desired topic truly is a good fit for the occasion. Only accept if you can speak with enthusiasm and credibility on a topic that is appropriate for the situation and audience, and if you have the bandwidth to prepare properly.

When the desired speech topic doesn't speak to your passions, interests, or expertise, suggest related topics that do. If you can't find a topic that works for both you and the event organizer, politely decline. Don't worry about upsetting the person who invited you. It would be far worse to accept and do a disservice to the audience and event, than it would be to decline. To soften the blow of declining, you might suggest other speakers you know and respect who could do justice to the topic.

THE AUDIENCE

Once you have identified a general topic that meshes with your interests, experiences, or expertise, focus on tailoring your topic to the listeners. Note that audience adaptation is not the same as pandering. The former has to do with framing your message in a way that will resonate with listeners; the latter has to do changing your message to appeal to a particular audience. Pandering is neither advisable nor ethical (see chapter 10 for details on ethics).

Tailoring your message to your audience requires thinking about how you can share your passion, experience, or expertise in a way that will be valuable to your audience. It's the process of making your presentation about them, and not about you.

Take for example, a how-to speech given by Kristi Saporito in an advanced public speaking course at The George Washington University. An accomplished softball player at the university, Kristi initially wanted to talk about her beloved sport. In thinking it through, however, she realized that fellow upper-level students in her course wouldn't gain much from learning about the rules of softball or how to form a recreational team.

Instead, she identified a problem facing her peers that was related to her passion for physical fitness: soon-to-be graduates likely would find themselves on tight budgets without access to a free gym (as they have on campus). Kristi gave a dynamic and memorable speech on how to get a good workout in a small space with inexpensive equipment. She brought sample equipment and demonstrated exercises that focused on various major muscle groups. It was a topic that struck the perfect balance between her passion and the needs of audience members.

THE SITUATION

Lastly, don't overlook the situational demands of your presentation. When you are presenting as part of a class or mandatory training program, be aware that your listeners are, to some degree, reluctant. Granted, they signed up for the class and ostensibly have a desire to learn. But, in many cases, learners are required to take and attend classes. As such, the bar for engaging listeners is higher than if audience members had sought out an opportunity to hear you speak. You must be particularly sensitive to the needs, desires, and problems of listeners if you want them to tune in to you, rather than Facebook or Instagram.

There also are cases when the occasion calls for a public address and you have been selected to speak. Your topic must be authentic to your interests, responsive to the needs of the audience, and sensitive to the demands of the rhetorical situation.

Consider the 2007 commencement address given by former U.S. Rep. Norm Dicks at the University of Washington, the congressman's alma mater. He focused his remarks on the work he and others were doing to restore the ecosystem of nearby Puget Sound. While appropriate for a speech at an environmental conference or a hearing on appropriations for federal cleanup efforts, it missed the mark for a graduation address. In fact, audience members were jeering and one student even ran on stage and made a gesture indicating to Dicks that he should wrap it up. (And it didn't help that he spoke for 15 minutes while it rained at the outdoor venue.)

The congressman made the speech about himself, rather than about the students on their graduation day. The genre of commencement addresses calls for congratulating graduates and those who supported them, acknowledging the challenges facing graduates, and inspiring in them hope and motivation to surmount those challenges and made a positive mark on the world. Sure, Dicks could have woven in a message about environmental stewardship and told related personal stories within the larger framework of a graduation speech, but he didn't. He made a policy speech about his interests without considering the needs of audience members or demands of the situation.

When you have the freedom to select a topic on which to present, there isn't a standard recipe for topics that always work. Don't search the Internet and don't give a presentation you gave in a different context. Select a topic that best fits the speaker, the audience, and the occasion, and there is a good chance that you will satisfy all three!

EXERCISE

When attempting to select a topic, the worst thing you can do is Google "speech topics." The results will be unoriginal and, most likely, not something interesting to you. Instead, be methodical in investigating a few ideas. Here's a way to do that:

1. List five of your interests that you think might even remotely connect to the type of presentation you have been asked to give.

2. Next to each of those topics, write key words, a possible thesis, a specific name, or place that connects with that topic: anything that will aid you in creating a more focused search for resources.

3. Give yourself a set amount of time to do initial research on each topic (somewhere between 10 and 30 minutes). Use the topic and the keywords to search for information that might help you construct a topic. Keep a document open on your computer and keep track of the different things you read. You don't want to waste time reconstructing a search or going through your browser history trying to find that great article you read but didn't save.

4. Evaluate which topic seemed best suited to you (the speaker), the audience, and the occasion. Consider the timeliness of the topic, your interest in it, the interest of the audience, the appropriateness for the occasion, etc.

Having a plan for topic creation limits the amount of time you might waste by just clicking links and following random leads. Once you have a topic, create a new document and begin culling information from the sources you already found. Now your presentation is on its way!

ACTIVITY

Think back to a presentation you gave that did not resonate with you (the speaker), audience members, or the situation. What was the context? What did you say? What went wrong? What could you have done differently to make the speech a better fit? What will you do differently when you are preparing for future presentations? ▪

—————— CHAPTER 14 ——————

WHAT YOU SAY
General Purpose and Thesis

Business communication consultant Dianna Booher hit the nail on the head when she said, "If you can't write your message in a sentence, you can't say it in an hour."

It seems simple and obvious. But when many professionals and students are asked to give the one-sentence version of their speech, they can't articulate a succinct main point. They get so focused on the trappings of crafting a presentation—stories to tell, facts to cover, charts to share, props to incorporate—that they overlook a basic, but necessary step in the process: identifying a general purpose and thesis.

GENERAL PURPOSE

Many public speaking texts classify speeches as having one general purpose, such as to inform or to persuade. But the general purpose is better understood as a ratio between a primary and secondary (and perhaps even tertiary) purpose. After all, most persuasive pitches do some informing. And a commencement address is mainly celebrating the accomplishments of the graduates and their supporters, but also could have an inspirational quality.

Remember that it is common to have more than one general purpose. Just make sure to identify the ratio (e.g., primarily persuasive and secondarily informative) and consider its appropriateness given the speaker, audience, and occasion (see chapter 12 for more on analyzing the audience and situation). In the event you are speaking in a classroom or learning environment, the general purpose of your presentation likely is spelled out in your speech assignment.

Here are some potential general purposes a speaker might have for a presentation:

TO INFORM

Informative speaking is aimed at enlightening listeners. It can provide a description, definition, demonstration, or combination thereof, and can come in the form of a briefing, report, training program, or other educational session.

When your primary goal is to inform, consider ways to make your material relevant, comprehensible, and memorable. Ask yourself: Why should listeners care? How does my subject pertain to their lives or interests? What metaphors, analogies, or other comparisons can I make to help audience members understand this concept? What mnemonic device might I use to help listeners remember main points or steps in an important process? What visuals can I use to show my audience what I mean?

TO PERSUADE

Persuasive speaking has the goal of changing the attitudes, beliefs, or actions of audience members. It is the heart of most public speaking courses and central to the success of many professionals, whether they are trying to land a job, secure a raise, sell a product or service, pitch an idea, win an argument, or change a policy.

Aristotle understood the importance of persuasion way back in the 4th Century BCE. In fact, he wrote an entire treatise, *Rhetoric*, to classify all of the available means of persuasion that a speaker has at his disposal.

Efforts to persuade often center around facts (such as a person being guilty or innocent, or Oswald acting alone in the assassination of President John F. Kennedy), values (such as favoring security over privacy, or one work of art over another), or policies (such as the worthiness of universal health care or suggesting that all undergraduates should be required to take a public speaking course).

If you are preparing a persuasive presentation, it is important to ask: How will audience members benefit personally by accepting the position? Where do listeners stand on the issue and how far can I reasonably change their position in the time allotted for my speech? What can I do to bolster my credibility? How can I make listeners care about my topic? How do I make the strongest case for my argument?

TO CELEBRATE

Celebratory speeches often occur at important rites of passage in life—like a milestone birthday, graduation, wedding, anniversary, retirement, and even death. These special occasion speeches are important opportunities to let the special people in our lives know how much they mean to us.

When crafting a speech with a primary purpose of celebrating a person or honoring his or her accomplishments, ask yourself: How can I succinctly explain my connection to the subject? What characteristics of the person are worthy of praise and what anecdotes highlight those traits? Who else needs to be thanked or acknowledged for helping this person reach his or her achievements? How can I situate this person's accomplishments into a larger context and give them greater meaning to the community of listeners?

TO INSPIRE

Managers, executives, politicians, military brass, and other leaders may find that they must deliver an inspirational and motivational message at moments of crisis. Sir Winston Churchill, the prime minister of the United Kingdom during some of the darkest days of World War II, immediately comes to mind (his 1940 "Blood, Toil, Tears and Sweat," is a great place to start if you are unfamiliar with this famous orator). Inspirational speaking also can be seen among headliners at industry conferences, self-improvement seminars, and school assemblies.

If the focus of your presentation is to motivate or inspire, consider asking yourself: How do I want audience members to approach life differently when they leave my presentation? What personal experiences and inspiring stories of others can I draw upon to connect with listeners? How can I reveal a personal fault or flaw in my story that will provide a poignant lesson to my listeners?

TO ENTERTAIN

Entertainment often is a secondary or tertiary purpose of presentations—think of a humorous how-to speech or Stephen Colbert's 2011 commencement address at Northwestern University. Though it is less common for the primary speech purpose to be entertainment, you can find this focus in after-dinner speeches, such as those given by the president and others at the White House Correspondents' Dinner, as well as roasts.

A SPEECH AIMED TO ENTERTAIN IS NOT THE SAME AS STAND-UP COMEDY.

Keep in mind, a speech aimed to entertain is not the same as stand-up comedy. The former is a speech with an introduction, body, and conclusion; the latter is a series of one-liners. Also, audiences bristle at mean-spirited jokes; the most effective type of humor is self-deprecating.

When preparing a speech to entertain, ponder these questions: What is my underlying theme or message? Who will get the humor (is it only for a few insiders)? How can I include some jokes at my own expense? Would my aunt or uncle be offended by the humor or language? How can I make the humor relevant to the listeners and what they care about?

THE THESIS

Every speech has a primary (and possibly secondary and tertiary) purpose; it gets at what you are trying to do in your speech: inform, persuade, celebrate, inspire, or entertain. Don't confuse this with your message: what you are trying to say in your speech. This is your thesis, and also can be called the specific purpose, central idea, or controlling idea. Your thesis should be a simple and singular sentence.

SIMPLICITY

The ideas contained within a presentation do not need to be simple, but your expression of these ideas does. Unlike the written word, listeners can't easily revisit a sentence in a speech that they don't understand.

Once a presentation is given, it usually disappears into the ether. If an audience member is confused or can't remember a key point, he or she doesn't have the luxury of rewinding the presentation. Sure, presentations can be recorded. But do you really want your audience needing to re-watch it in order to understand it? Chances are, they won't go back. And ironically, the speeches that audiences will seek out to watch again are simple, straightforward ones that they connected with, remembered, and liked the most.

How do you achieve simplicity in your thesis statement? Keep it short and direct. Avoid using a comma, "and," or other grammatical tool to connect ideas. Distill your message to its most basic form.

SINGULARITY

Your presentation should have laser focus. The topic must be narrow and specific. Otherwise, you risk a presentation that gives breadth but no depth.

To tell listeners something they don't know, have them understand it, and get them to remember it, you must drill down on a topic.

An undergraduate student and Disney aficionado, Monica Caporaso, wanted to give a three- to four-minute informative speech overviewing the Walt Disney World Resort in Florida. Her thesis was: I will inform my classmates about Disney World's history, key attractions, and how to plan a trip there. The commas as well as the "and" were giveaways that her thesis lacked both simplicity and singularity. How could she have done justice to those topics in one minute each? When it comes to your speech thesis, less is more.

WHEN IT COMES TO YOUR SPEECH THESIS, LESS IS MORE.

Monica could have selected any one of the three topics in her original thesis to pursue for her informative speech. She decided to revise her thesis to the much simpler and more specific statement: I will inform classmates about the two newest attractions at Disney World. Not only was it more laser focused, Monica's thesis also was more relevant to audience members who already visited the attraction but did not know about the latest and greatest rides.

One last word of advice when it comes to a thesis statement: be sure to take Dianna Booher's advice to articulate your thesis in a sentence (as opposed to a word or phrase). If Monica had said for her thesis "Disney World attractions," it would not necessarily have been clear to audience members that her primary purpose was informative. Having a sentence-long thesis ensures that you identify a primary general purpose (ideally basing it on a careful analysis of the context of your presentation) as well as a simple and singular subject.

Lastly, don't squish a thesis and preview together. Unlike what you might have been taught in high school or college writing classes, separating the thesis and the preview is a good idea when giving a presentation. You want to present your important information in digestible and memorable pieces. A main idea combined with a multi-clause preview of the key points in a speech is less likely to stick in the minds of the audience. Separate the two.

EXERCISE

Pretend you are about to deliver your upcoming presentation, but have just been informed that the program is running behind and you have to deliver your message in an abbreviated fashion. Give a one-minute version of your speech. Then, give a 30-second version. Finally, distill it to one sentence. If you do not overtly say this one sentence in your speech, incorporate it (ideally after your attention getter and in your introductory material). For some persuasive speeches, this key line may best come at the end of your speech.

ACTIVITY

Think back to a memorable speech – one that has left a lasting impression on you – that is recorded. Before reviewing the speech, write down its simple and singular thesis. Then, identify what you believe the primary, secondary, and even tertiary general purpose of the speech is. Now, watch the recording of the speech. Do you still have the same understanding of the thesis and speech purpose? If you had the same understanding, what about the speech helped you remember? If you have a different understanding of the thesis or purpose of the speech after revisiting it, why do you think it has changed? How can your responses inform your preparation of future presentations? ▪

—— CHAPTER 15 ——

WHAT YOU SAY
Research

The process of learning more about a topic is the process of research. Research should not be thought of as finding stuff to plug into spots in a presentation. Nor should it be thought of as a formulaic process that yields consistent results if a series of steps are followed. Research is more like the scene in Lewis Carroll's *Alice in Wonderland*, when Alice follows the rabbit into the rabbit hole and emerges in an entirely different world. Once you begin researching, the process should take you to different and unexpected places.

It is impossible to know exactly how the research process will go. Your topic, the occasion, and the audience will dictate the process in important ways. However, here are some tips to to guide the research process so that you do not feel like you are floundering:

FIRST EFFORTS

Assuming you are researching a new topic, it is important to resist becoming overwhelmed with information. Toward that end, designate a set amount of time—30 minutes is a good amount in most cases—to conduct basic web research. The primary goal during this time is to identify how you will use the rest of your time to research. You may start to understand how little or how much information is available, what the key terms are that will help focus your research, and who the most prolific authors or sources are.

During this initial 30 or so minutes, you might have a sheet of paper out or a document open on your computer to record key terms, names, sources, dates, etc. If you find a website that seems particularly helpful, bookmark it or cut and paste the URL into your notes. But don't go too far down the rabbit hole just yet.

The benefit to setting a time limit is three fold. First, it sets a manageable goal at a time when you might feel overwhelmed by the task at hand. You can do anything for a half hour. Second, it forces you to stop and evaluate how you will proceed. Third, it avoids a long, dark descent into digressions that might be off topic or unproductive (which will likely feed the feelings of being overwhelmed).

CONSTRUCTING AN EFFECTIVE SEARCH

With the notes and knowledge you have gathered from your First Effort, you now need to create specific searches. Searches should always begin as specific as possible. This helps curtail the glut of information that might come if you type in the terms "Japan" and "economy" when searching for information about current monetary policies in that nation. A better option would be to search "Japan," "monetary policy," "(the current year)," and the name of a key figure from the Japanese government—a detail you might have gathered in your First Effort.

Another strategy when searching is to use different search engines. Google uses a proprietary algorithm to search the web. Microsoft's Bing uses a different one. And so too does Yahoo. You might be surprised what appears on the first few pages of search results when using different search engines.

In addition to searching with different engines, take advantage of specific filters that many search companies have created. The most prominent example is Google. If you wanted to search for current news on specific medical procedures, you could click on the "news" link in the banner on Google, and your search would only return information from news sources. Without this, your search might return dozens of results from wikis, general sites on Japan or currency, or capital-management companies. In addition to news sources, one can narrow results to books, patents, or peer-reviewed academic articles. Using filters can help avoid unwanted search results.

USING YOUR LIBRARY'S RESOURCES MIGHT SEEM OUTDATED—"I CAN FIND IT ALL ON GOOGLE"—BUT FOR TOPICS BASED IN ACADEMIC OR PROFESSIONAL PUBLICATIONS, THE LIBRARY IS STILL THE GATEWAY TO ACCESSING THAT INFORMATION.

Searching within aggregators and content-specific websites is another good strategy for expanding yours research base. If you attend a university, your library pays for subscriptions to information that is not freely available. Many academic journals, newspapers, and trade publications can only be accessed in full-text format through subscription. Aggregators are companies that buy the access rights to publications. Using your library's resources might seem outdated—"I can find it all on Google. Why go to a library?"—but for topics based in academic or professional publications, the library is still the gateway to accessing that information in a free, full-text format. It also is a great place to get assistance with your research from a trained librarian, who can help if you have done your due diligence and are still struggling to track down key documents or types of information.

EVALUATING CREDIBILITY

Not all research is created equal. You might find a source that says exactly what you were looking for, but the information was from an anonymous comment on an intensely biased website. This information is not credible, right?

Well, it depends. Any piece of information can provide credible support for the right claim. For example, if you were writing an informative briefing on the newest cell phones, factual reporting from a technology news website would seem better than a story from your grandmother. However, if you wanted to make the point that a particular phone was easy to use, that point might be best supported by the anecdote from a less technology savvy source (time to quote granny).

The basic questions of credibility are: Does this source have the authority to say what they are saying? Will my audience accept his or her authority on the topic? If the answer to either question is "no," consider whether the information should be in your presentation or think about how you can frame the information to turn the "no" into a "yes."

Ultimately, the process of research is like an apple. The skin of an apple, while edible and full of important nutrients, is not enough to sustain a person. Your First Effort is the skin of the research apple.

Most of an apple is made up of the flesh of the fruit. This is delicious and yields the most filling part of the apple. The time you spend executing your plan after the initial 30 minutes of your First Effort search is like the flesh of the research apple.

The inner most portion of the apple is the core, which contains the seeds. The core, while not a part that most people think about eating, is essential to the apple. Its role is underappreciated, but essential for the fruit's longevity. The few very specific facts, figures, or examples that you search for and find in the research process are the seeds. They go underappreciated because they end up being a relatively small part of the overall speech, but without them, the speech would be lacking and might not make the strong impression that you want.

Remember to think about research as a process. Doing so will allow you to stay open to the *Alice in Woderland*-esque twists and turns in your research that will lead you to the discovery of useful and interesting information to include in your presentation. What is the result of this research journey? A better supported, more authoritative presentation.

EXERCISE

Find a Wikipedia page for a potential speech topic or a subject that interests you. Not all Wikipedia pages are created equal, so what you are looking for is a page that is detailed, that is not flagged for being potentially biased, and that is thorough in its citation of sources. Rather than stopping your research at this point, click on source links at the bottom of the page or search for a few of the cited sources. What is the benefit of using Wikipedia entries as a jumping-off point and tracing its footnotes for your supporting material? How does it impact your credibility?

ACTIVITY

Watch *An Inconvenient Truth*, the 2006 documentary film about former Vice President Al Gore's efforts to increase awareness about global climate change. What types of supporting material does Gore use in his presentation, both verbal and visual? Is this supporting material credible to you? Interesting? Why or why not? ▪

—————— CHAPTER 16 ——————

WHAT YOU SAY
Supporting Material and
Sources of Information

Now that you have a handle on the overall research process, you might be asking what material you should pull from research to use in your speech and the most authoritative places to find that material. The aim of this chapter is to overview the types of supporting material you can use in a presentation and the most likely places to find it.

Remember to select different types of supporting material to bolster your credibility as a speaker as well as the points you plan to make in your speech. Variety is the spice of life; and when it comes to supporting material and sources of information, it helps keep presentations interesting too.

FACTS AND STATISTICS

Facts are verifiable pieces of information and statistics are numerical facts. Though key facts and statistics can provide useful grounding in a speech, avoid overdoing it. Some speakers get bogged down with only this type of supporting material because they think they should stick to "hard evidence." But when used to excess, facts and statistics quickly become impersonal and boring. Ideally, this type of supporting material should be brought to life with examples, stories, and narratives.

Also, be careful with your use of statistics. Remember that they are predictions based on mathematical probability and shouldn't be treated as certainty. They also can be misused, mischaracterized, or manipulated, so make sure that you get statistics from a primary source (and not a newspaper article or blog that is summarizing the original data) and check for consistency among similar studies (don't cherry pick an outlier statistic to make your case).

Furthermore, avoid making assumptions about specific groups of people based on statistics (the rate of HIV among your classmates likely differs from national averages). And avoid generalizing statistics beyond the population that was surveyed (attitudes toward employer-sponsored 401(k) programs among factory workers in Michigan may not hold true for colleagues at your consulting firm).

Facts and statistics are helpful in informing audiences about an issue or problem as well as diffusing emotional or controversial topics.

COMPARISONS AND CONTRASTS

By making comparisons in a presentation, you try to add meaning to one thing by highlighting its similarities with another. Analogies (when you compare two things with the words "like" or "as," such as "clean as a whistle") and metaphors (when you compare two things without using such words, as in the example "the world is my oyster"), are two common types of comparisons. Contrasts, on the other hand, seek to emphasize the difference between concepts.

Comparisons and contrasts are especially useful in helping listeners understand unfamiliar concepts, think about known concepts in a new way, and make sense of abstract material.

EXAMPLES, STORIES, AND NARRATIVES

Examples describe a specific instance to help illustrate a point. They can be quite short or extended, factual (based in reality) or hypothetical (believable, but not rooted in one lived experience). They differ from stories in that they don't develop like a story—with a beginning, middle, and end. Examples are dime a dozen in political speeches; just watch a U.S. president's State of the Union address for examples of people who have been helped by government initiatives or who stand to benefit from policy proposals. Examples are a great way to make an abstract issue more concrete for audience members.

SPEAKERS MUST BE CAREFUL NOT TO FILL THEIR PRESENTATIONS WITH STORIES FEATURING THEMSELVES AS THE HERO.

Stories, on the other hand, are more developed than examples. They are a recounting of events that include five elements (that you may remember from English class in middle or high school): setting, plot (action), characters, conflict (a problem), and a theme (moral). Refer to chapter 17 for more on why stories are so effective in presentations and how to tell them well.

Stories are memorable, interesting, and can evoke emotion in listeners. But speakers must be careful, however, not to fill their presentations with stories featuring themselves as the hero. This can come across as self-centered and boastful. Instead, the personal stories you share should reveal vulnerability or a weakness, credit people or experiences that helped you find your way, and offer an insightful lesson.

Stories and narratives commonly are used synonymously. But John Hagel, director of Deloitte Consulting LLP, made a useful distinction between the two in his presentation at the 2013 South by Southwest Interactive Festival. He argued that narratives differ from stories in two important ways:

> One is that narratives are open-ended. They don't have resolution. There is something that is in the process of unfolding. The end is yet to be determined. And second, there's an invitation to all of us to participate in that narrative, to help determine what the outcome is going to be.[1]

Take for example the American Dream: With ingenuity and work hard, anyone in the United States can be prosperous and successful. Sure, we've heard the life stories of U.S. presidents Abraham Lincoln and Barack Obama, which are completely different, yet both consistent with this narrative. But the American Dream narrative itself is broader; it is situated culturally and helps define the identity and values of a group of people.

When presenters evoke this narrative, it can lend powerful support and can become a persuasive argument for listeners to take a specific course of action (such as buying a product, changing a habit, or voting for a candidate in an election). Thus, while examples and stories are interesting and memorable, tapping into deep-rooted narratives can be an effective way for speakers to motivate audience members to take action—often a difficult thing to do.

TESTIMONY

A written or spoken statement qualifies as testimony. We often think of it in terms of testifying in court, but you are using testimony as supporting material whenever you quote an expert or lay source in a presentation.

QUOTING A LAY SOURCE CAN BRING AN ISSUE TO LIFE BY INTRODUCING THE OPINION OR PERSPECTIVE OF A PERSON WITH WHOM AUDIENCE MEMBERS CAN RELATE.

Expert sources have academic, professional, or experiential knowledge that gives them special standing to speak on a topic. On the other hand, lay testimony generally is the opinion of an average person on a topic—think of so-called "person-on-the-street" interviews. For example, if you were giving a speech about the merits of flood insurance, you might include expert testimony from an insurance adjustor as well as lay testimony from an average homeowner in your area.

Testimony can help explain a concept or phenomenon to listeners. Rather than using a dictionary definition or Wikipedia entry, cite expert testimony.

Quoting a lay source can bring an issue to life by introducing the opinion or perspective of a person with whom audience members can relate.

Now that you have a sense of the types of supporting material you can use in presentations, where should you look to find them?

BOOKS

Once a mainstay of research, books (and visits to the library) have fallen out of favor with many students and professionals who find online searches more convenient. But, don't overlook the bounty of supporting material that can be found in books—any of the types listed above, depending on the publication. You now can expedite a trip to the library by conducting Internet searches to find relevant books at your school, organization, or local library, or to place a request to get a useful book delivered to your preferred location from a consortium library. Another convenient option may be an e-book, which you can download to your computer, tablet, or e-reader. E-books can offer a low-cost or even no-cost way to get a book without having to step foot in a library.

Note that with the proliferation of self-published books and e-books, you should be cautious about the veracity of information printed in these books. Something edited and published by one of the big U.S. publishing houses (Simon & Schuster, HarperCollins, Random House, or Penguin Group) or by a publisher that is reputable in a specific academic field (like SAGE in the field of communication), provides some assurance that you can rely on the information in a book. But don't dismiss self-published books, which have already taken over a significant market share from traditional publishers. To decide whether a self-published book contains trustworthy information, you might check the expert credentials of the author, note if the author carefully cites material from outside sources, and look for formatting errors and typos (a sign that the research conducted for the book might be sloppy too).

ACADEMIC JOURNALS

These publications are filled with scholarly articles written and peer reviewed by experts in their respective fields. Published on a quarterly or monthly basis, they offer in-depth, original research that has been thoroughly vetted. Look to such studies for facts, statistics, and expert testimony. Remember to look at the works cited in such articles to find other excellent sources of information; this is called citation chasing.

GOVERNMENT PUBLICATIONS

The U.S. government is a prolific publisher of information. From transcripts of congressional hearings and floor speeches delivered by members of the U.S. House and U.S. Senate to original reports from agencies like the U.S. Census Bureau, U.S. Bureau of Labor Statistic, and the U.S. National Highway Traffic Safety Administration, among many others, government publications offer a treasure trove for researchers looking for reliable sources of examples, stories, expert testimony, facts, and statistics.

MAGAZINES

Generally produced more frequently than academic journals, magazines offer more in-depth coverage of issues than newspapers, but are published in a more timely fashion than journal articles. This means they can be quite reliable sources for facts, testimony, comparisons, contrasts, examples, and stories of recent phenomenon.

Remember, most magazines don't present original research, but they report on interesting studies that are published elsewhere. It is fine to use a magazine to find an academic study; just make sure you track down the primary source of that research to ensure that you are accurately characterizing it and not relying on someone else's summary of it. This advice holds true for other secondary sources that report on original research, such as newspapers, wikis, websites, blogs, and social media.

NEWSPAPERS

These daily publications are filled with concise articles that are written by reporters and edited by newspaper staff. They offer the best way to find information on recent news and events, especially expert and lay testimony, examples, stories, and even facts. Take care to track down primary sources of information (like facts and statistics) that are reported in newspapers but originally published in other sources.

WIKIS AND REFERENCE BOOKS

Wikis are the online and populist version of traditionally published reference books. They allow contributors to write, edit, and delete content on specific topics. Wikis, and famously Wikipedia, are a good way for researchers to get an introduction to an unfamiliar subject and to find additional sources of information to explore on that topic. Because wikis are crowd sourced and the ones that are edited often can't keep up with contributions to entries, they should not be relied upon as sources of information in a presentation. They can, however, be used as a means of citation chasing; most cite articles from journals, newspapers, magazines, as well as other sources of primary information. Because reference books are edited and published, the veracity of information is more reliable. But, they are still secondary sources of information; find primary sources to bolster your credibility as a researcher and presenter.

WEBSITES

Many academic journals, government publications, magazines, and newspapers are now accessible online (and in some cases are available before print editions hit newsstands). But for the purposes of this discussion, websites are considered sources of information that exist only online.

The diversity of material on the Internet is indicative of the diversity of supporting material you can find on websites. But a word of caution: as is the case with self-published books, websites run the gamut in terms of quality and credibility. Look for websites that have a transparent sponsor (the organization behind the site); pages that have a named author with sterling credentials; a date when the page was posted, published, and updated; thorough citations; and polished writing, grammar, and formatting.

BLOGS

Blogs (a shortened version of "web logs") are online diaries that typically display entries or posts in reverse chronological order. But personal blogs are just the tip of the iceberg—blogs cover topics as diverse as health and fitness to personal finance, travel and dining to technology, news and politics to fashion. Researchers can use blogs to find comparisons, contrasts, examples, stories, and testimony. Blogs may even summarize and link to primary sources of facts and statistics. Remember to approach blogs like other websites—taking care to check for signs of quality and credibility mentioned above.

SOCIAL MEDIA

Social-media networks are online platforms that promote the creation and exchange of user-generated content. Including the likes of Facebook, YouTube, Twitter, Instagram, and Pinterest, researchers might tap into social-media sites for examples, stories, and lay testimony to include in presentations. Additionally, such sites may be utilized to obtain breaking news on current events before other sources can publish them.

The next time you are conducting research, select a variety of supporting material to bolster your credibility and the points you make in your presentation. Aim for variety in supporting material and sources of information to keep your presentation fresh. ▪

---

1. Hagel, John. "Moving from Story to Narrative." SXSW Interactive Festival. Hilton Austin Hotel, Austin, TX. 11 March 2013. Conference Presentation.

——— CHAPTER 17 ———

WHAT YOU SAY
Storytelling

Facts, statistics, testimony, examples, and comparisons are useful forms of supporting material that you can collect during the research process. These nuggets of information can help listeners understand your message and make sense of new concepts. Such material can add color to a speech and, if fully explained and cited, can bolster your credibility.

But alone, these forms of supporting material can fall flat because audiences don't connect to them emotionally—something even Aristotle knew was an important aspect of persuasion when he included pathos (appeals to emotion) in his artistic forms of proof, along with ethos (appeals regarding the speaker's credibility), and logos (appeals to logic) in his classical treatise *Rhetoric*.

More contemporary communication theorists also extoll the virtues of storytelling. In her 2010 book *Resonate*, Nancy Duarte described the power of stories:

> Ever since humans first sat around the campfire, stories have been told to create emotional connections. In many societies, they have been passed along nearly unchanged for generations. The greatest stories of all time were packaged and transferred so well that hundreds of illiterate generations could repeat them. Our early ancestors had stories to explain day-to-day occurrences in nature such as why the sun rises and falls, as

well as more overarching metanarratives about the meaning of life. Stores are the most powerful delivery tool for information, more powerful and enduring than any other art form. [. . .]

Information is static; stories are dynamic—they help an audience visualize what you do or what you believe. Tell a story and people will be more engaged and receptive to the ideas you are communicating. Stories link one person's heart to another. Values, beliefs, and norms become intertwined. When this happens, your idea can more readily manifest as reality in their minds. (16)[1]

Duarte goes on to lament that most speakers simply deliver reports. She argued that presentations aren't just reports; they are a middle ground between reports (facts, figures) and stories (drama). They are explanatory and must have data woven into a compelling story that drives the presentation and keeps it interesting.

Communication theorist Walter Fisher went even further when he explained the importance of narratives. He posited in his landmark 1984 essay, "Narration as a Human Communication Paradigm: The Case of Public Moral Argument," that humans are *homo narrans*—that our essential nature, what separates us from other animals—is the fact that we are storytellers.[2]

PRESENTATIONS AREN'T JUST REPORTS; THEY ARE A MIDDLE GROUND BETWEEN REPORTS (FACTS, FIGURES) AND STORIES (DRAMA).

Maybe he's right. After all, just think of how much we love stories—children love listening to stories from books as well as family lore, especially the story of how their parents met or when they were born; older kids and young adults get engrossed in chapter books and teenagers especially tune into the daily dramas of their friends' lives; and adults find joy in reading a page-turner by a favorite

WHAT STORY SHOULD I TELL?

The best storytellers can tell a yarn about the most mundane of life experiences (just listen to any great comedian for proof). But if you're new to storytelling, focus on signature stories—narratives about the moments in your life that were eye-opening and helped shape the person you are today.

These "ah-ha" moments don't have to be momentous in a public sense—you don't have to win a prestigious award or accomplish a longtime goal (though such events may very well be fodder for signature stories). A signature story may come at any time you have an epiphany, like the ones told by Steve Jobs in his 2005 commencement address at Stanford University.[3]

When you are preparing a speech and have your thesis and main points identified, think of what story or stories will help you make your case. Look first to your signature stories and other personal narratives. Also, consider telling compelling stories about other people you know, or even those you have read about, heard on the radio, or seen on television. You may even know of a fable or myth that would help make a point in your speech.

As you identify and refine your stories, remember that each should have a beginning (where the setting and characters are introduced), a middle (where a conflict or problem unfolds and reaches a climax or turning point), and an end (where the conflict is resolved and closure is provided). We all have a friend who, when he or she tells a story, gives information out of order, never gets to the climax, or who abruptly ends a story without warning or closure. Most of these problems can be solved by paying attention to the general form of a story and practicing your delivery.

author, and find refuge in stories told in movies, television shows, and even music lyrics.

We make sense of experiences not by recounting facts, but by telling them as stories with characters, conflict, resolution, and a moral. Why then, if stories are so pervasive in our lives and experience, do so many speakers hesitate to share them in presentations?

Some speakers question whether listeners want to hear a story about their life. Maybe it is too personal or revealing. Others object by saying stories are "fluff" and opt to use solely empirical data.

Don't fall victim to these false assumptions. In fact, listeners love relevant stories that serve as supporting material in well-researched and crafted presentations. The more personal a story is, particularly when the storyteller reveals a fault or shortcoming, the more connected audience members feel to a speaker. And on message stories aren't a waste of time in a presentation. Too many facts and figures will cause the eyes of listeners to glaze over. But some carefully selected data, paired with a powerful narrative on the topic, will help make your point and help listeners remember it long after they leave your presentation. When considering supporting material for your next speech, don't overlook the power of stories.

EXERCISE

Patricia Fripp, a professional speaker and speech coach, suggested the following five foolproof storytelling prompts.[4] Use them as prompts to practice telling personal narratives, and possibly, to identify some of your own signature stories.

1. "I wish you could have been there . . ."
2. "I'll never forget the time when . . ."
3. "It wasn't exactly what I expected . . ."
4. "It was one of the most exciting days of my life . . ."
5. "It was the scariest moment of my life . . ."

ACTIVITY

Watch a recent State of the Union Address. How did the U.S. president weave stories into this annual report to Congress on the nation's state of affairs? Which stories resonated with you? Which didn't? What differentiated stories that worked from stories that didn't? What lessons can you draw from your analysis that will inform your telling of narratives in future presentations? ▪

1. Duarte, Nancy. *Resonate: Present Visual Stories that Transform Audiences.* (Hoboken, NJ: Wiley, 2010). Print. 16.

2. Fisher, Walter R. "Narration as Human Communication Paradigm: The Case of Public Moral Argument." *Communication Monographs* 51 (1984): 1-22. Print.

3. Jobs, Steve. "Steve Jobs' 2005 Stanford Commencement Address (with intro by President John Hennessy)." *YouTube.* 14 May 2008. Web. 8 November 2013.

4. Fripp, Patricia. "A Day with Patricia Fripp." Monthly Meeting. National Speakers Association Washington, D.C. Area Chapter. Bethesda Marriott Hotel. Grand Ballroom. Bethesda, MD. 22 May 2010. Conference Presentation.

—— CHAPTER 18 ——

WHAT YOU SAY
Main Points

We've all done it. You have a presentation to give. It is supposed to be a casual report on a project with which you are very familiar. You tell yourself, "I know this better than anyone. I'll just go in and we will have a conversation about it." Then, when you walk in and begin presenting, you start repeating yourself, you return to previous points to fill in details you left out, you remember an important point that probably should have been said first. In the end, you realize that although you conveyed all of the information that you wanted, it was rough.

Constructing main points, even when you are confident about the material, is important both for you and your listeners (and for the same reasons). You and audience members want a clear message that has a purpose, is well-explained, logically structured, and confidently delivered. Constructing main points plays a big role in achieving these ends.

HOW DO I CREATE MAIN POINTS?

If you are not quite sure what you are going to say to support your thesis, try writing down all of the ideas that you have on a sheet of paper or typing up a list. Once you have recorded all of your ideas, you will probably notice that some ideas can be combined, some ideas that seemed important don't really fit with the others, and some ideas seem to relate to others in specific ways.

After you have brainstormed, review your points and ask yourself if there are any points that need to be added or deleted. In making these decisions, consider how the points relate to:

- Your purpose
- The substance of the point
- The composition of the audience
- The expectations of the occasion

Taking these considerations into account, you might decide that because of the advanced knowledge base of your audience, that a point about the background of your project would be unnecessary. Or you might decide that because your purpose is to report on quarterly performance, that suggestions for future actions might be a subject for a different time (or, perhaps, a brief mention in the conclusion rather than a main point).

At this point, you might find it helpful to assign the ideas a tentative order in the speech by numbering them or moving them within the document that you are typing. This raises the next question in creating main points.

IN WHAT ORDER SHOULD I PUT MY MAIN POINTS?

You may have a tentative order in mind, but it might be helpful to think about a few patterns of arrangement that could suit your presentation. There should be a reason why your points occur in the order that they do.

The general factor to consider is whether or not your points are logically independent or dependent. Logically independent ideas do not rely upon each other. Each point individually supports the central idea of the presentation. If another point is weak, it has minimal impact on the other main points. Logically dependent ideas build upon one another in a chain-like fashion. You need each link in the chain to be strong or the central idea will fall flat.

Here are just a few patterns of arrangement:

TOPICAL

Also called categorical, this pattern of arrangement selects independent categories that are related to a theme, but not necessarily like links in a chain. If you are reporting on the sales performance of three products, your main points might be: Product A, Product B, and Product C. Although there will probably be a reason why you place these three topics in a specific order, logically you could place them in any order and still meet the purpose of your presentation.

CHRONOLOGICAL

The benefit to organizing a presentation based on time is its linearity. Time is very orderly, which can help an audience understand the connection between points. Most people think of chronological as past, present, and future, but a chronological arrangement can also use eras as its markers of time. Additionally, there might be a reason to change the order. Perhaps you are speaking about the impact of a recent policy on your business's profit. You might begin with the present to note how profits have risen, and then return to the past to show how they got to that point, before addressing what action needs to be taken in the future to ensure that profits continue to rise. If you are using chronological order to set markers of time, your points logically are logically independent. When you move into past, present, and future (or some variation thereof) for a persuasive speech, you likely have logically dependent points—meaning that if listeners don't accept earlier points, they will not accept latter points.

SPATIAL

Spatial organization moves from topics that are most distant from your audience to those that are closest. For example, a presentation that discusses changing market forces impacting your business might begin with European market forces, then move to U.S. market forces, and then arrive at local (state or county) market forces. To audience members living in that state or county, you have taken them from distant, yet important factors, while gradually covering topics that are closer to their daily lives. This type of organization generally is logically independent—each "stop" on your speech journey can stand on its own.

PROBLEM-SOLUTION

In problem-solution reasoning, order matters. We don't take action to solve non-existent problems. There are too many other issues that require our attention and resources. In general, if a presenter has done a poor job demonstrating the significance of a problem, an audience is not likely to endorse a plan of action, no matter how simple or feasible it is. This is an example of speech points that are logically dependent.

CAUSAL

Like problem-solution, a cause and effect structure requires a close connection between points to yield the greatest impact. For example, what causes the greatest growth in the U.S. economy? Is it reducing taxes? Is it increased taxation with increased government subsidization and reinvestment? Is it a reduction in export regulations? To prove that any one of these is the cause of an improving economy (i.e., the effect), the reasoning must be compelling.

PROCESS OF ELIMINATION

One of the more undervalued patterns of reasoning, this form of reasoning presents a series of points, eliminating each before moving to the next one, upon arriving at the last point, which will be the best option. The benefit of this pattern of reasoning is that it allows the audience to understand how the eventual best option was decided. The speaker, like a third grade math student, is showing their work. When audience members feels like they were reasoning alongside you, their confidence in the decision will be stronger. Because listeners must accept the arguments you dismiss before arriving the best option, points structured this was should be considered logically dependent.

NOW WHAT?

The last step in constructing main points is to run a few tests.

SUBORDINATION AND BALANCE

First, look at the main points and ask if they are equally important? This means that each main point is worthy of being a main point and is not better suited as support for another main point. If a main point seems to fit within another main point, this subordination means that it was not worthy of main point status. Another part of judging whether points are equally important is balance. This also means that main points have roughly the same amount of content. If one main point takes five minutes to explain, and the other two main points take two minutes each, the speech will seem very top heavy and the significance of the latter points will seem like afterthoughts.

COORDINATION AND DIVISION

Second, ask yourself if the main points are being team players? Like being a member of a team, each main point should work with the other points to achieve a common goal. They must coordinate with one another. But, also like being on a team, the main points should each contribute something unique to the effort. If two main points do the same thing, the main points are not clearly divided.

CLARITY

The last question is, do these points make sense? Take a breath, or if you can, take a day away from your presentation. Then come back and look with a fresh set of eyes and ask, will these main points make sense to my audience? Sometimes our attention to detail can blind us to the most obvious—and important—big-picture questions.

EXERCISE

Watch a famous oration on www.americanrhetoric.com. As you listen, identify the main points in the speech. What pattern of arrangement was used? Where points logically independent or independent? How did the arrangement of main points add to or detract from the speaker's overall message?

ACTIVITY

Craft a Sandwich Structure of a three to four minute speech on a hobby or interest. The topic could be anything from knitting to photography, cooking to soccer. It should be something that you know well and are passionate about. You may have already done this activity back in chapter 11 on the Sandwich Structure. Feel free to revisit that outline, or start from scratch if you haven't already crafted one.

Identify two different patterns of arrangement that you could use for your main points to support a speech on this one topic. In each arrangement, are the points logically dependent or independent? In what situations would one pattern of arrangement be more helpful to listeners than the other you identified? What pattern of arrangement might be more conducive to recalling your main points while speaking or to crafting creative presentation aids? ▪

CHAPTER 19

WHAT YOU SAY
Signposting and Transitions

When an instructor or trainer provides a list of the main points to be covered in class and clearly states when they are moving from one point to another, do you appreciate the clarity? When another educator seems to jump from point to point, do you feel lost and frustrated? The source of your gratitude or frustration in these situations can be attributed the use of signposts and transitions.

SIGNPOSTS

Signposts are verbal cues that communicate the structure of your presentation to audience members. Much like traffic signs, you want these to be clear, consistent, but not so intrusive that they hurt rather than help the flow of your material. To ensure that your presentation has signposts but also flows, transitions are needed. To continue with the transportation metaphor, transitions are like the merging area on freeway on-ramps. It is jarring to enter a freeway with too little time to merge. Likewise, it can be jarring for a listener to move from one point to another without understanding the connection between the two. Signposts are critical for keeping an audience alert and ensuring the points in a presentation flow smoothly.

The first instance of signposting occurs after your attention getter, thank-you's, thesis statement, and any brief expository material (like definitions or background on a topic). This is the preview of main points. It occurs when you explicitly state the main points of your presentation. In the preview, use parallel structure to make it pop. Parallel structure means that each point in the preview is constructed in the same way. Think about the number of words and the grammatical structure. For example, if you were giving an informative briefing about the history of a local coffee shop, you might offer the following as your preview: "Today, I will discuss the establishment, the development, and the future of Stumptown Coffee." If you preview your main points in this way, you hope that your audience catches that your main points are:

1. Establishment

2. Development

3. Future

By labeling each main point as one word, the main ideas are clear and easy to recall.

PREVIEW

A preview lets your audience know where the presentation will go; however, it is not time to begin giving the information about the stop along the way. Over previewing can be identified by the presence of a conjunction: "because," "therefore," and "however" are a few common ones. If we take the above example, over previewing might sound like this: "Today, I will discuss the founding because the story behind it is so interesting, the development, and the future, which is bright." The extra verbiage is a barrier to letting the parallelism do its job and make the preview overt and memorable.

Also important is to continue to use the phrasing from the preview when signposting throughout the presentation. You might think that repeating the same words and phrases throughout the presentation is redundant. It is, but the repetition is important for clarity and audience retention. If you decided to start using synonyms or change the phrasing—perhaps you signpost your second point as "building the company" instead of "development" in the above example—your audience might wonder if this is part of the first point or the second. Using consistent language throughout your signposting greatly reduces the likelihood of such confusion. Rest assured, being repetitious is a virtue in a presenter and not a vice (as is often the perception in written work).

USING CONSISTENT LANGUAGE THROUGHOUT YOUR SIGNPOSTING REDUCES THE LIKELIHOOD OF CONFUSION.

TRANSITIONING

The type of signposting that takes place after the preview and in the body of a speech is called transitioning. Transitions can occur within one sentence or can take several sentences (particularly in longer presentations). Transitioning between main points of a presentation involves three elements: internal review, link, and internal preview. An internal review wraps up the previous point (often using your signpost from that point). A link that connects the previous point to the next point. The link should explicitly or implicitly provide a reason why you are going to the next point. And an internal preview states what the next point is. For example, when transitioning from the "founding" to the "development" points in the coffee shop speech, one might say, "From its establishment in 2002, Stumptown Coffee was an immediate success. But the owners asked themselves how they would continue to innovate and grow the business. That's why the company implemented a development strategy, the main prongs of which are customer engagement, new products, and social responsibility."

REVIEW

Finally, when you have concluded the body of your speech, don't forget to review your main points. Remember the old saw, "Tell 'em what you're gonna tell 'em, tell 'em, tell 'em what you told 'em?" This is when you tell 'em what you told 'em – you review the main points using the same verbiage that now will be recognizable to listeners.

In the example of the coffee speech, the review can be as simple as, "Today, we have discussed the establishment, development, and future of Stumptown Coffee." Keeping the wording of the review consistent at the end of your presentation will offer one last opportunity to help audience members commit your main points to memory and to signal that your speech is coming to a close. Yet another benefit of reviews, when done in conjunction with a clincher (see chapter 20 for more on clinchers), is that they help prevent the awkward moment at the end of a speech when listeners are not sure if a speaker has concluded and if they should start clapping for him or her.

BEWARE OF GOING OVERBOARD IN A SHORT, SIMPLE SPEECH—BY OVERDOING SIGNPOSTING AND TRANSITIONING, YOU CAN COME ACROSS AS TOO BLUNT, TOO OBVIOUS, OR "LISTY."

Signposts should occur at key junctions in a presentation: after the introduction of a speech and before the first main point, between main points, and after the last main point and before the clincher. All presentations should have previews, transitions between ideas, and reviews—even short impromptu speeches. But the level of detail you provide in your signposts should scale up as your presentation gets longer or more complex. Beware of going overboard in a short, simple speech—by overdoing signposting and transitioning, you can come across as too blunt, too obvious, or "listy." But when used together in balance with the type of presentation you are giving, signposting makes for a clear, fluid presentation for which audience members will be grateful (and not confused or frustrated).

EXERCISE

When was the last time that a friend, coworker, or family member asked you "how was your weekend?" or "what did you do on your trip?" It probably happens frequently. Use these common conversational questions to practice signposting and structuring your response. Answer such questions without listing a slew of details. Mark the highlights by signposting your reply. An answer might be "On Friday night. . .," "Then Saturday. . .," and "On Sunday. . . ." Or, "The three favorite attractions I visited during my trip to Washington, D.C., were the White House, the Lincoln Memorial, and the Library of Congress." How could you use signposting to respond to a likely question you will get during an upcoming meeting or following an upcoming presentation? Practice your signposted response.

ACTIVITY

On October 24, 2009, Barack Obama delivered the first major address on health care during his presidency. Watch the speech (www.whitehouse.gov/video/President-Obama-Address-to-Congress-on-Health-Insurance-Reform). Try to track the structure of the speech. What are the words or phrases that helped you identify when a new idea is being introduced? How did Obama use signposting to make a lengthy and complex speech more digestible for listeners? When he could he have employed more effective signposting during the speech? Identify one section that needs better signposting and rework that section of the speech. ▪

—————— CHAPTER 20 ——————

WHAT YOU SAY
Attention Getters and Clinchers

"Ezra . . . jump. Ezra . . . jump. Ezra . . . jump," whispered Justin Solar, an undergraduate public communication student who was delivering a speech of tribute to his grandfather. His listeners were hooked. No electronic gadget or thought of what was for lunch could distract audience members from Justin's every word.

During his speech, Justin chronicled the incredible story of his grandfather Ezra. It was 1940. Ezra, who was then just eight years old, was instructed by his mother to jump off a moving vehicle that was driving him and his family to sure doom at a concentration camp in Poland. Ezra jumped, escaped his Nazi captors, survived on his own in the woods of Poland for four years, became the sole Holocaust survivor from his nuclear family, and later immigrated to the United States where he started his own family.

Justin led with a suspenseful hook to an unforgettable and haunting story, which he then linked back to in the conclusion of his presentation to bring his speech full circle. He exemplified the value of a well-crafted attention getter and clincher.

Sure, having a catchy introduction and conclusion adds interest, but why are attention getters and clinchers vital to the success of a presentation? The law of primacy and recency states that people best remember what they hear first and last. When applied to presentations, it means you want to speak first or last in a series of speakers. More importantly, it means you want the introduction and conclusion of your presentation to shine. Here's how you can make sure they do:

INTRODUCTIONS

Most effective presentations open with an Attention Getting Device (AGD) like Justin's, a controlling idea or thesis (see chapter 14 for more on developing one) and a preview (see chapter 19 for a thorough discussion of signposting). It is not hard to see why these factors would aid in communicating effectively: you want the attention of audience members, you want to make your message clear, and you want to provide a roadmap to explain how you will support that message.

THE FIRST WORDS OUT OF YOUR MOUTH ARE THE MOST IMPORTANT. THEY SET THE TONE FOR YOUR ENTIRE PRESENTATION AND DETERMINE WHETHER MEMBERS OF YOUR AUDIENCE WILL TUNE YOU IN OR TUNE YOU OUT.

Don't make the common mistake of underestimating the importance of the AGD. The first words out of your mouth are the most important. After all, they set the tone for your entire presentation and determine whether members of your audience will tune you in or tune you out. Don't wing your opening lines (a common mistake). Painstakingly develop, script, and memorize each word. You only need a sentence or two with this level of preparation, but doing so will ensure the first words out of your mouth are purposeful and powerful. This will hook your audience, give you confidence, and get your presentation off to a strong start.

In addition to the AGD, thesis, and preview, other information may be necessary to set the stage for the rest of your presentation. Orienting material—basic information that the audience needs to know to be able to understand your thesis—is sometimes necessary. For example, if you were reporting to a credit union board of directors about how a federal law impacted such financial institutions, your orienting material might include a few sentences about the history and status of the Federal Credit Union Act. Orienting material is not all of the background on a subject, but just enough to provide the most basic amount of knowledge listeners need to understand your message, or to explain an acronym or technical phrase that is important to your thesis.

In addition to orienting material, you might also include a statement of significance in your introductory remarks. Statements of significance express the urgency of the issue that your presentation will cover. For example, a presentation to a group of college students about the need to invest in their retirement might fall on deaf ears. It might sound as if you are one of their parents or grandparents lecturing them. But, if in the introduction you swiftly explain the tens of thousands of dollars more they can earn if the begin investing at age 22 instead 30, then perhaps the students would perk up and listen.

DO'S AND DON'TS FOR YOUR AGD

As always, these are general rules that, in the right situation, can and should be broken. But when in doubt, follow these guidelines:

USE STORIES

Sharing an anecdote will pull your audience in. After all, everyone loves a good story. In fact, the communication theorist Walter Fisher argued humans should be called *homo narrans* because the essential difference between us and other animals is that we are storytellers. Personal stories are great; compelling stories about other people or dramatic hypothetical situations can work too. (Refer to chapter 17 for more on storytelling.)

USE SUSPENSE

Getting people to anticipate what's next is an effective way to keep them engaged. Suspense can go hand-in-hand with telling a story in your speech opening, as was the case with Justin's AGD. Suspense also can be achieved by asking a rhetorical question, making a promise to your audience that you'll fulfill in the course of the speech, or saying a series of seemingly disparate words and later explaining their relationship or importance.

USE SAYINGS

Consider sharing a funny or thought-provoking quotation to open a presentation. Avoid clichés and make sure to attribute the saying to the correct author. A good place to look for inspiration and to identify sources is *Bartlett's Familiar Quotations.*

USE SHOCK FACTOR

Too many statistics or facts can make listener's eyes glaze over. But one that is well-documented, relevant, not-widely-known, and shocking can hook an audience in the first moments of a speech. Make sure it is simple and easily understandable; consider incorporating a visual aid to compliment what you are saying.

USE SELF-DEPRECATING HUMOR

Humor isn't easy to pull off and it's not for every speaker. But a joke, especially one relevant to the speech topic and made at the expense of the speaker, can both grab attention and win over an audience in the beginning of a speech.

And here are a few words of warning. Avoid these common mistakes that speakers make when starting off a speech:

DON'T REITERATE YOUR NAME, SPEECH TITLE, OR TOPIC

Don't squander the first sentence your speech doing something that an emcee should do for you. Script a one-minute introduction of your presentation. Include your name, a brief description of your credentials on the topic, what your audience will get from listening to you, and your speech title. (See chapter 29 for more on introducing a speaker.) Get the introduction to the event organizer well ahead of time and bring a hard copy for the emcee, just in case he or she doesn't have it. The introduction of a speaker should never be the same as the opening line of the presentation.

DON'T START BY THANKING THE AUDIENCE OR HOST

It often is appropriate and important to acknowledge event organizers, hosts, sponsors, attendees, and other dignitaries in your audience. Just don't do it first thing. Hook your audience with the first sentence or two of your speech, then say your thank yous and continue with your introductory material.

DON'T SPEAK BEFORE YOU COMMAND THE ROOM

Avoid uttering a sound before you've taken your place at the front of the room, waited for applause to end, adjusted the microphone, arranged your notes, taken a drink of water, and looked around the room with a smile on your face. There is nothing that undercuts a speaker or shows a lack of confidence more than talking on the way to the lectern or rushing to start. You need to feel comfortable before you can start strong. Take your time, own the room, and then begin your speech.

DON'T LET "UM" ESCAPE YOUR MOUTH FIRST

After you command the room, you don't let "um" or another junk word slip out before your start your first sentence. The opening of your speech should be the most rehearsed part. It might even be memorized. Every word should be said slowly, crisply, and purposefully. Think through the words in the first sentence that should be emphasized and any gestures that would add impact.

There's no room for "um" before or during a well-prepared opening line.

A corollary to this is to not let your first words be nervous banter. Don't tell the audience how nervous you are or that you are a terrible public speaker so they need to bear with you. In rare moments, this can be integrated as part of an attention getting strategy, but most of the time it makes the speaker seem lacking in confidence. And as a consequence, greatly diminishes his or her credibility.

CONCLUSIONS

Surely, the opening lines of a presentation are crucial, but don't give short shrift to the concluding lines. After all, the law of primacy and recency suggests that leaving a positive last impression is as important as leaving a positive first impression. The last line of a speech should signal the end of the presentation and conclude the speech in a powerful, memorable way.

When writing your so-called clincher, aim to return to your AGD. In the case of Justin's tribute speech, his conclusion linked back to his grandfather's courage to jump as an eight-year-old boy, how it was indicative of the way Ezra lived his life, and how we all should draw strength from the story so we too can leap metaphorically when confronted with difficult moments in our lives.

No matter how you open your presentation, effective concluding lines often re-evaluate the AGD in light of the information that was communicated in the presentation. If you opened with a startling statistic—for example, the number of people in the United States who do not have clean drinking water—your clincher might remind the audience of this number and suggest that if they take the action you specify, that number hopefully will be zero someday. The benefit of returning to your AGD in the conclusion is that it brings the presentation full circle—you are dropping off your listeners where the tour started, but with much more information than they previously had.

Some presenters will offer a call to action for their audience and use that as a clincher. The call to action is a great strategy for directly connecting the presentation to your audience. Other presenters are drawn to sayings or quotations as a way to clinch. These can be effective, so long as the saying or quotation is not trite and is relevant to the presentation. For example, it might seem odd to end an informative briefing on pothole repairs with a quotation from Martin Luther King, Jr. or Mahatma Gandhi.

No matter what you choose to do in the clincher, it is imperative that it provides a definitive and clear end to the presentation. If you have done your job, you won't need to say "Thank you" or "That's the end" because your audience already will know that you have concluded and you will end on a high note.

EXERCISE

Most people have a favorite vacation destination. It might as simple as staying home or as glamorous as traveling abroad. Imagine you are telling a friend about this place. Write an introduction that captures your enthusiasm, builds toward a thesis, and ultimately captures the attention of your friend. This intro should be no more than 30-45 seconds, so it should develop relatively quickly.

ACTIVITY

Think about your favorite movie. It probably had a scene early in the film that captured your attention or an ending that was memorable. What are some lessons we can take from film or literature that might apply to opening or concluding a presentation? ▪

—— CHAPTER 21 ——

WHAT YOU SAY
Complementing with PowerPoint and Presentation Aids

If you learned to snow ski as a child, you likely started without poles. They can be distracting and overwhelming to novice skiers. Even worse, they can provide a false sense of confidence and can even prevent you from leaning how to stop and turn properly. Your ski instructor likely didn't allow you to use poles until you fully mastered the fundamentals and were ready to tackle more advance ski techniques.

The same principle holds for presentation software, such as Microsoft PowerPoint, its Apple-product cousin Keynote, and newer arrival Prezi. Like novice skiers clinging to their poles, many novice speakers cling to such presentation aids as a crutch—a crutch that encourages you to write your presentation on slides and read it to your audience with little or no rehearsal.

Surely, ski poles are useful for intermediate and advanced skiers; and presentation software can be for speakers who are ready to tackle more advanced presentation techniques. Whenever possible, you should learn the fundamentals of effective presentation delivery and content before graduating to the use of presentation software. If you add PowerPoint and other programs to the mix too soon, you may find that, like ski poles in the hands of novice skiers, this aid can be more of a liability than an asset.

When you are feeling ready to use presentation software in conjunction with your next speech, here are a few maxims to guide your thinking:

QUESTION WHETHER YOU NEED IT

American business culture has come to expect a slide deck with every presentation and that mentality has permeated academia, government, and non-profit sectors as well. But many of the most powerful speeches are given without a single presentation aid. (Dr. Martin Luther King, Jr.'s "I Have a Dream" speech is an obvious example, though one that occurred before the advent of presentation software. A more recent example of then senatorial candidate Barack Obama's 2004 keynote address to the Democratic National Convention also comes to mind.)

EVEN IN SITUATIONS WHERE PRESENTATION SOFTWARE WOULD BE APPROPRIATE OR EXPECTED, CONSIDER BUCKING THE TREND OF USING IT ANYWAY.

In some contexts, like table-top briefings or sales pitches where a speaker is presenting to several listeners at the same table, using presentation software would be awkward at best. Worse, it could hinder the process of building rapport with audience members, making them less receptive to new ideas or calls to action.

Even in situations where presentation software would be appropriate or expected, consider bucking the trend of using it anyway. Doing so can help your presentation stand out from the crowd of speakers who use it and can bolster your credibility by showing you don't need to rely on slides to deliver your material.

And avoiding presentation software doesn't mean you can't use presentation aids. You can still incorporate aids into your speech such as posters or handouts of graphs, charts, diagrams, photographs, and other images; physical objects that serve as props; live demonstrations of a process or procedure; clips of music, videos, or other audio-visual material. Just make sure that visuals look professional and are large enough for everyone to see (whether you do them or hire a copy shop to help), and that audio is loud enough for everyone to hear. These lower-tech alternatives to presentation software can be just as effective (if not more so because you aren't likely to create posters of just text) and less stressful because there is a smaller chance of technological difficulties.

PRESENTATION AIDS SHOULD SUPPLEMENT, NOT REPLACE THE PRESENTER

If a listener can get everything he or she needs from the screen or a handout, then you, the presenter, have reduced your value and utility. Audience members can tune you out, read your materials, and not miss a thing. You effectively made yourself obsolete and created competition for the attention of listeners. Worse yet, you likely insulted your audience members by assuming they need someone to read text for them and by wasting their valuable time.

Instead, use presentation aids to elevate the presentation. They should help listeners understand and remember your message. For example, if you are discussing the voting trends of college-age students over the last 50 years, the numbers could get very confusing if presented only orally. But, a simple, well-labeled and described line graph would allow audience members to see and grasp your point immediately. And if you are establishing your credibility on the subject of traveling abroad, it would make your case more memorable, interesting, and believable if you showed several photographs of your foreign adventures as you explained the highlights. Images complement the verbal and will work together to make your presentation more memorable.

If you decide to use presentation software, think of it as a relatively easy and effective way to incorporate presentation aids. Not to say that you might not run into technological difficulties (and Murphy's Law says you will), but when such programs work as intended, they are a fantastic way to project graphs, charts, diagrams, photographs, pictures, and audio-visual clips for a large audience to see.

PRESENTATION AIDS ARE FOR THE AUDIENCE, NOT THE SPEAKER

Don't make the mistake of using presentation aids, and especially presentation software, as notes. You certainly may take an outline or other materials to the lectern to speak from, but these materials should never be available to listeners on a screen or on a handout! And if you must provide a client or listener a stand-alone document as a report, create a different set of slides for your oral presentation. Rest assured, the presentation you speak from does not have to be the same as the handout or written report you provide listeners. On the contrary, it can be useful to think of presentation aids as a supplement to a written document that is meant to breathe life—with videos, pictures, and stories—into the facts and data on paper.

When selecting presentation aids to include in your next speech, ask yourself: Does this presentation aid add something that could not be conveyed with words alone? Is there a story that would come alive or a piece of information that would make more sense if paired with a presentation aid? If you answered yes, include it. If you are including the presentation aid because it will serve as a prompt for what you want to say or so that it will fill up white space, leave it out.

Once you have decided to use presentation aids and have settled on a format (hard copy or electronic), you then should turn your focus to designing them. Here are some general guidelines for what a presentation aid should look like.

COLOR

Generally, stick to soothing colors. Yellows, oranges, and reds signal alarm and danger (think street signs). Blues, greens, and purples are more soothing colors.

Also, consider how the use of color impacts the ability to read content. Putting yellow, orange, or red text on a white slide renders the text virtually invisible. And text (including white text) on a black or dark background is very difficult to read. You can't go wrong with black or dark text on a white background. It is standard fare for a reason: it is easy to read.

COMPOSITION

Though applicable to posters and other materials that are printed in hard copy, it is especially important to be aware of composition in the design or theme of the slides in presentation software. Each type of presentation software has its own selection of templates and slide themes. In choosing one, remember that it should be appropriate for the situation (your purpose, the audience, the situation). Picking something "cute" might be fun for a friend's birthday party or the boss's roast, but should not be the impulse for everyday business (unless you are in the business of cute).

PICKING SOMETHING "CUTE" MIGHT BE FUN FOR A FRIEND'S BIRHTDAY PARTY OR THE BOSS'S ROAST, BUT SHOULD NOT BE THE IMPULSE FOR EVERYDAY BUSINESS (UNLESS YOU ARE IN THE BUSINESS OF CUTE).

The second dimension of composition is words on the page (or slide as it were). A common rule for composing text on a single presentation slide is the 4x4 Rule: Have no more than four bullet points, and each point should be just four-words long. This rule of thumb is particularly useful for presenters who are chronic cut-and-pasters, or for presenters who tend to use slides to aid their speaking rather than the ability of listeners to understand and remember.

The 4x4 Rule can be broken. Shoot, you are encouraged to break it, so long as you think carefully about how to make your slide effective. If, for example, you wanted to quote five sentences from an external reviewer's report of your organization, you would NOT place that text on a slide and then instruct your audience to read it while you talk. This forces a choice between you and the visuals, yet often leads to audience's selecting a third option: tuning out. Instead, you could read the first sentence aloud. Then, paraphrase the next four sentences, providing enough time in your paraphrasing for the audience to read the rest of the paragraph. By guiding your audience through the presentation aid, you are able to use the information to its fullest potential while also maintaining the attention of your audience.

Lastly, protect white space. One of the most brilliant web pages is the homepage for Google. It is the word Google with a search box beneath it, centered in the middle of a sea of white. Crisp, simple, and singular. Apply these principles to your presentation aides and slides; avoid filling them up with too much stuff. Less is more when it comes to visuals.

COORDINATION

It goes without saying that the presentation aid should hang together as a cohesive whole. There is rarely a reason to infuse a different design scheme, font, color, animation, etc. into the middle of a presentation. It would not coordinate with the rest of the presentation and would serve only to interrupt the flow.

PRESENTATION AIDS, LIKE ALL PARTS OF A PRESENTATION, NEED TO BE REHEARSED

Now, let's cover the basics of successfully incorporating presentation aids:

PRACTICE

Whether you are using presentation software, a poster, a prop, or other material to supplement your speech, you must practice with it. Start incorporating your presentation aids during your early rehearsals so you can use them confidently, fluidly, and automatically. There's nothing worse than fumbling through a demonstration or finishing a presentation only to realize that you forgot to advance your slides or display the objects you intended to show. But if you don't rehearse, it is easy to get flustered or forget in the moment, when nerves are running high.

WHAT PRESENTATION SOFTWARE SHOULD I USE?

Technology changes rapidly. To offer you in-depth advice on how to use specific presentation software programs and technologies would render this chapter useless before it is printed. Thankfully, human evolution works much slower than software development. That is to say, the principles about what to do with the technology have not changed because how the human brain processes information will not dramatically change from the moment we write this to the time you read it.

But for those who are new to presentation technology, here is a quick introduction. The phrase "presentation software" overwhelmingly connotes Microsoft's PowerPoint software. It has, by far, the largest share of the market with one billion people worldwide using Microsoft Office, the suite of applications that includes PowerPoint, Word, Excel, and other programs. In the early 1990's Microsoft created this easy-to-use slide presentation tool. It is much like the old days of overhead projectors; except where you once would have manually changed the transparency, you now click the mouse on your computer.

Though PowerPoint dominates the market, Apple has an alternative program called Keynote. Still based on the idea of advancing slides, Keynote does provide users a few more options for animation than PowerPoint. And for presenters who want to try something different or are in creative fields where the linearity of PowerPoint and Keynote might not be as effective, there are other options.

A notable newcomer is Prezi (www.prezi.com). In March 2013, the web-based presentation software hit the 20-million-user mark and continues to attract new users at a rapid rate. Launched in 2009, Prezi is favored by many TED-style speakers, who are known for presenting bold ideas with compelling stories in a dynamic delivery style.

According to the Prezi website, the cloud-based presentation software has a "zoomable canvas [that] makes it fun to explore ideas and the connections between them." It is like working on a digital whiteboard, where you can add text and images to support points in a presentation. As you move through the presentation, you can zoom into each of those visual elements to provide listeners more detail and then you can pan back out to put points into the big-picture context.

Prezi provides worthy competition to the longstanding domination of slide-based presentation software and merits the consideration of presenters who want to try something different.

SHOW THE ENTIRE ROOM

When you practice with and use presentation aids in a speech, make sure everyone can see them. Check to ensure that all audience members can see a screen that is projecting your slides. If you opt for a prop or poster, make sure it is large and clear. Then, walk across the front of the room slowly and purposefully as you describe it so listeners have ample time to take it in. Do this in practice because it feels awkward to hold a presentation aid for a minute or longer. All too often, speakers hold up a presentation aid and put it down too quickly when they are nervous. This belies anxiety and undercuts all the work that went in to carefully identifying or crafting a useful presentation aid.

DON'T LET THEM BECOME A DISTRACTION

If one extreme is putting a presentation aid away too soon, some speakers have the opposite problem: they keep it out past the point of usefulness. In the case of presentation software, this means leaving text or an image on the screen after you move on to another point. When a visual doesn't sync with the spoken word, listeners can become distracted. That's why you should advance to a relevant slide or to a black placeholder slide to help focus the attention of listeners.

Similarly, if you are using a poster to supplement your speech, don't continue displaying it on an easel after you make your point. Put it flat on a desk or turn it around so the blank side is facing listeners. And just as importantly, don't continue to hold a prop in your hand after you have discussed it—you might start gesturing with it, which is quite distracting. Instead, put it on the lectern or another place where you won't be tempted to pick it up and fidget with it when you are nervous.

MAKE SURE THEY ARE EXPENDABLE

Technology will fail at some point (remember the Clinton story from chapter 1?). Perhaps you forget a power cord for your laptop. Perhaps there is not a cord to connect your computer to the projector. Perhaps the lamp burns out on the projector. Perhaps you drop your prop on the way to your presentation and it breaks. Perhaps a sudden rain shower ruins your poster. No matter how conscientious you are, something can and will go wrong with your presentation aids.

As important as a presentation aid might be to your speech, it is important to consider what you would do if you did not have it. Make sure you have a contingency plan for giving the speech without the presentation aid (that may mean printing out a hard copy of your PowerPoint slides or sending your file to an e-mail account that you can access last minute). After all, the show must go on. The hallmark of expert speakers is the ability to proceed with grace and confidence in the face of technological failures such that audience members never know there was a problem in the first place (ah-hem, remember the Clinton story from chapter 1?).

EXERCISE

Craft a three to four minute descriptive speech that paints for listeners a vivid picture of a person, place, or thing. Deliver and record your speech three times: once using presentation software, once using a non-electronic presentation aid (poster, picture, prop, etc.), and once with no presentation aids. Review the recordings. How did your delivery differ? What were the strengths and weaknesses of using electronic presentation aids, non-electronic presentation aids, and no presentation aids?

ACTIVITY

Watch "The Beauty of Data Visualization" by David McCandless (www.ted.com/talks/david_mccandless_the_beauty_of_data_visualization). How do visuals enhance the presenter's argument? What are the main lessons about using visuals to represent complex ideas? ▪

CHAPTER 22

WHERE YOU SAY IT
Rehearsals

Aristotle is credited with saying, "We are what we repeatedly do. Excellence, therefore, is not an act, but a habit."

This is especially true when it comes to presentation skills. If you want to achieve excellence as a speaker, rehearsal is vital. It may seem obvious, but in years of coaching students and clients, we have found that many speakers don't know how to rehearse.

A case in point is that of work-life integration coach Carolyn Semedo. She was preparing a speech for a small-group coaching session and on the day she was set to deliver it, recalled feeling frustrated that she still was stumbling over the content of her presentation.

She chalked it up to being a mediocre presenter. When asked how many times she had practiced, she acknowledged that she'd done two rehearsals, including one in the car on the way to class.

Of course Carolyn's delivery was rocky! Even the most celebrated speakers don't have their material down on a third run through. On the contrary, the speakers who make public speaking look easy are those who have practiced their craft and their material the most.

The dirty little secret of public speaking is that most speakers are nervous and most speeches are bad because presenters do not rehearse nearly enough. **So, how many times should you rehearse? At least six.** That's right, a minimum of six times.

There is something special about the sixth rehearsal. It is the rehearsal when speakers command their content, can recover quickly from hiccups in their delivery, and feel significantly more comfortable at the lectern. (To remember how many rehearsals, just think, "six sticks" or "six for success.") Very few speakers rehearse this much—a likely reason why so many speakers are anxious about giving speeches and why so many speeches are underwhelming.

Now you know how many rehearsals you need to do. But what exactly should you do and expect each time you practice?

REHEARSALS 1 AND 2

For these initial practices, speak from a well-researched and carefully crafted outline. (While the focus here will be on how to rehearse from a detailed outline using the extemporaneous mode of speaking, many of these recommendations apply when it is necessary to read from a prepared text.) It's not advisable to start rehearsing before you have completed your research on the audience and situation (see chapter 12 for details), established a concrete messaging strategy (see chapters 13 and 14 for details), and developed a working draft of your speech outline (see chapter 11 for details).

But, don't wait until your outline is perfect to start rehearsing—you'll put it off too long and won't have time for all your rehearsals. Start rehearsing when you are at 85 to 90 percent ready with your outline. Don't worry; you can still make adjustments to the content of your speech in your initial rehearsals. And, it will be better to give a speech where both the content and delivery are at 85 percent ready than one where the content is at 100 percent and the delivery is unpolished. A good rule of thumb is to start rehearsing about a week in advance for a presentation.

For your first two rehearsals, speak sitting down in a comfortable spot. Don't worry about your delivery style; focus on the content of the presentation— getting familiar with it and identifying where you need to edit for clarity, style, and length.

During your initial rehearsals, expect a rocky delivery that comes in fits and starts. You likely will find it difficult to explain points clearly and concisely; transitions will be rough. Don't start from the beginning every time you make a mistake. Get in the habit of continuing your presentation. After all, it is good practice for hiccups that might occur before an actual audience.

DESPITE THE POPULAR ADVICE TO PRACTICE IN FRONT OF A MIRROR, AVOID THIS TECHNIQUE. IT CAN BE UNNECESSARILY DISTRACTING.

Use a stopwatch to determine whether you have significantly too much or too little material, and edit your speech right away. It is never a good idea to ignore time constraints or plan to rush through material to fit it in your allotted time. You may also find in these first rehearsals that you need to edit the arrangement of some points to make the presentation more coherent or to add stories to add color to facts and figures.

REHEARSALS 3 AND 4

For your next two rehearsals, continue working off the outline you edited after your initial rehearsals. Now, aim to deliver your speech from a standing position. It doesn't need to be formal—standing up in an empty conference room or even your bedroom will do.

Despite the popular advice to practice in front of a mirror, avoid this technique. It can be unnecessarily distracting. Instead, wait to videotape and review footage of a later rehearsal or your dress rehearsal to identify areas where you can improve your delivery.

Expect to be more fluent with your material on the third and fourth rehearsals. But don't be surprised when you go blank and can't remember what you wanted to say, or struggle with the wording of ideas or the transitions between points. This is normal. You might make some notations on your outline during these rehearsals, but avoid making major changes to the content or to the notes you will speak from (as you will develop a memory of where things are on your outline so you can find your point easily).

Continue to practice with a stopwatch. You can expect more consistency with the length of the speech and the timing of specific parts, such as the introduction, main points, and conclusion.

REHEARSALS 5 AND 6

For the fifth and sixth rehearsals, speak from the outline that you should know well at this point. Now, deliver your speech standing behind a lectern or with a setup that closely resembles the speaking situation you will encounter on presentation day.

Expect to feel more comfortable with your presentation. It will come off your tongue much more easily at this point. You will start to form patterns in the way you say certain parts of the presentation, though each time you say it will be a little different because it is not scripted or memorized.

Now that you are gaining command of your speech content, there will be fewer hiccups in your delivery. And when you do stumble, you will be able to recover much more quickly and gracefully.

Start to focus on your delivery (see chapters 3 to 8 for more detail). Turn your attention to avoiding speaking habits that will distract your audience from your message, like using repetitive hand gestures, swaying, or relying on junk words (e.g., "um," "uh," "like," "so," "you know," and any other word, phrase, or sound that only serves as a verbal crutch). This is when analyzing a video recording of your rehearsals is especially useful. You don't need fancy equipment; recording on a cell phone or computer is fine. Just make sure your device is close enough for your voice to be picked up and easily heard when you review the recording. Remember not to be overly critical of yourself. There is no such thing as a perfect speech or speaker, so don't hold yourself to this unrealistic expectation!

Keep timing yourself. Your rehearsals should be quite consistent in length, even without having to glance at your stopwatch during the run through.

REHEARSAL 7+ AND DRESS REHEARSALS

When you reach practice seven and greater, you have graduated to the dress rehearsal. For these fine-tuning sessions, continue to speak from your familiar outline. Don't change the format or mess with it now. You may not need to refer to your outline many times, but keep it with you. When you get nervous in your dress rehearsals and especially on presentation day, you will find yourself taking glances at it. There is no shame in having notes; it is undoubtedly better to pause and look down at an outline to get back on track than it is to struggle needlessly and awkwardly during a presentation.

DELIVER YOUR DRESS REHEARSALS AT THE LOCATION WHERE THE SPEECH WILL BE DELIVERED, WITH THE TECHNOLOGY ANS SETUP YOU'LL BE USING ON SPEECH DAY.

Deliver your dress rehearsals at the location where the speech will be delivered, with the technology and setup you'll be using on speech day. Most event organizers will be happy to accommodate your request for a dress rehearsal—they will appreciate your willingness to invest so much time and care in your presentation.

If for some reason you can't do an on-site dress rehearsal, deliver your final rehearsals in a setup that emulates presentation day as closely as possible. And take a few minutes at some point before you go on stage to case the location where you will give your speech. Even seeing the room, especially how the lectern and technology will be set up, can help reduce uncertainty and make you feel more confident going into your actual presentation.

For your dress rehearsals, focus on getting comfortable with the location and setup, as well as conveying enthusiasm in your speech.

YOU CANNOT CRAM REHEARSALS FOR A PRESENTATION. IT ALMOST NEVER WORKED FOR EXAMS IN SCHOOL, AND CRAMMING ALL SIX REHEARSALS INTO THE DAY (OR NIGHT) BEFORE A PRESENTATION WON'T WORK FOR THE VAST MAJORITY OF SPEAKERS EITHER.

Think about vocal variations, gestures, facial expressions, and dramatic pauses you can use to make your presentation more interesting and memorable. Again, recording and reviewing your dress rehearsals will help improve your delivery.

Don't forget to bring your stopwatch and remain aware of timing. It can take longer to deliver a speech with a microphone, particularly in a location with an echo. Also note that it generally takes longer to deliver a presentation

PRESENTATION DAY CHECKLIST

You have done the hard work of crafting and rehearsing a great speech. Don't leave anything to chance on the day of your presentation.

Here is a checklist of things to bring with you so you can perform at your peak:

- Notes and props you will use at the lectern
- Professional-looking folder to hold your notes
- Thumb drive with your PowerPoint or other supporting material in an electronic format (remember to send a copy to your easily accessible e-mail account as a backup)
- Handouts, brochures, or other materials you plan to make available to your audience.
- Evaluation sheet (if you plan to get written feedback from your audience)
- Video camera and related equipment (if you plan to record your speech and/or get audience responses to your speech on video)
- Business cards
- Pen (but don't hold it while you speak)
- List of stretches and vocal warm ups (see chapter 2 for details)
- Bottle of room-temperature water
- Light snack (such as fruit, an energy bar, or a bagel)
- Mints (and not gum)
- Medicine you may need (for headaches, upset stomach, etc.)
- Grooming supplies (comb, mirror, lip balm, makeup, etc.)

before a live audience because you pause while listeners react. Plan to have a time cushion; 10 percent of the total allotted time for the speech is sufficient. On a final note, you cannot cram rehearsals for a presentation. It almost never worked for exams in school, and cramming all six rehearsals into the day (or night) before a presentation won't work for the vast majority of speakers either. One or two rehearsals a day during the week leading up to your presentation is a good goal. If you are a novice presenter or have an especially nerve-racking speech, start even earlier and do more rehearsals.

Following a rehearsal schedule of at least six rehearsals may sounds excessive. But it means the difference between feeling unsure and uneasy like Carolyn, or feeling confident and comfortable at the lectern.

EXERCISE

Rehearse a speech six times in the week before you are scheduled to deliver it. Record your first and sixth rehearsal. Watch the videos and write down specific improvements in your delivery and content. Brainstorm ways you could make your final presentation even better. How did you feel during your first rehearsal versus your sixth? How was the process of rehearsing different from speech preparation you have done in the past? How did your preparation impact your level of confidence and your performance in your final presentation?

ACTIVITY

Interview a seasoned speaker you know and respect about his or her process for rehearsing formal presentations. What surprised you about the process? What insights can you apply to rehearsals for your next speech? ▪

—— CHAPTER 23 ——

WHERE YOU SAY IT
Briefings and Informative Speeches

It has been said that boredom is the deadliest poison. If true, then all too many informative speeches make the workplace toxic. But briefings don't have to be dry, technical, and boring. Employ the following strategies to make your material memorable and useful the next time you explain a process or problem to colleagues, update clients on a project, share insights with classmates, or report research findings.

GIVE YOUR AUDIENCE A REASON TO CARE

First, figure out why your message is important to your audience. Talk to several expected attendees and find out what they already know about the topic and how your subject impacts them.

Then, ask the all-important WIIFM question: "What's in it for me?" This requires you to consider how listeners stand to gain from your presentation. After all, humans are selfish; we want to know how we will benefit personally from listening to a presentation. Craft the central idea of your presentation accordingly; it should be relevant to audience members.

For example, you might be a great photographer who wants to give a presentation of your photos from a recent vacation. While interesting to you, this topic may be boring to listeners. But, if you frame the presentation as a how-to speech sharing your top three secrets for taking great photographs of landscapes, using your recent vacation photos as examples, you provide useful insights to audience members. Speeches should be a win-win situation: The speaker should get to talk about a passion and listeners should walk away with information that has practical value. To find this sweet spot, however, you must spend time analyzing your audience, their interests, and needs. (See chapter 12 for more about analyzing the audience and situation.)

STAY FOCUSED

When conducting briefings, fight the impulse to include everything. Instead of a saying a little on a lot of topics, have a clear and focused central idea that is relevant to listeners, supported by two or three key main points. This will make the material you do cover more understandable and memorable. Stay out of the weeds—keep the level of detail appropriate for the knowledge level of your average listener. Remember, a presentation should be about providing value to listeners, not demonstrating how much you know. People who want more detail can always ask during Q&A or talk with you one-on-one at a later time.

INCORPORATE A THEME

Especially for dry topics, introduce a theme that you can weave through your informative

TO LEAVE BEHIND OR NOT? WHEN AND HOW TO USE HANDOUTS.

Handouts often come with informative speeches. Many are a waste of paper. Others can be useful for increasing understanding and giving listeners something to refer back to in the future. But they must be done thoughtfully so they don't detract from your presentation.

First, think long and hard about the necessity of using a handout. For a short or straightforward informative speech, forgo them and send an electronic follow-up after the session if warranted. If you decide they are important for a longer or more complicated briefing, pay attention to what is on them and when you hand them out to maximize their utility.

If you do decide a handout would be helpful, you will want to include:

- Enough material for the audience to follow your presentation and take useful notes, but not so much that they could read it and replace listening to you. Handouts should supplement, not replace, the speaker.

- Room for notes. People will remember more if they can jot down ideas and put concepts in their own words. Double-sided handouts can include space for notes and save paper;

- Reproductions of visuals. If you have a complicated graph or other visual, include it in your handout so audience members can study it up close while you are explaining it.

- Additional resources. Because you can't cover everything, a handout is an ideal way to tell attendees how to reach you for more information, including how to connect by phone, e-mail, and social media, and other places to go to learn more, such as websites, books, articles, films, etc. You can also include material or appendices that have more detail than you can cover during your presentation. Your handout does not have to be an exact replica of your slides (and in many cases should not be the same).

When you use handouts, make sure to distribute them strategically.

Never pass out paper while you are speaking. The movement of people and sound of papers shuffling creates competition for attention (there already is enough with phones, tablets, and wandering minds). When your handouts include room for note taking or information that would be useful to have during the presentation, distribute them before your audience arrives (when possible) or before you begin your presentation. If the handout mostly contains resources and/or contact information, you might consider making it available at the end of your presentation for people who are interested in learning more.

speech. This will help you avoid the "info dump," whereby a speaker unloads vast quantity of information on their audience all in the name of being informative. If your audience cannot track your presentation or tunes out, is it really worth it?

Take for example, an HR professional who was preparing a speech for colleagues on an important reporting process that they only had to complete a few times a year (and often messed up, making her job much more difficult). An avid pianist, she linked each part of the process she was describing to one of her favorite piano pieces. Her listeners will never forget to submit their completed information with the online form . . . and hear Scott Joplin's "The Entertainer" in their heads while they do it. A good theme doesn't have to be overtly related to the content of the speech. It should, however, be creatively linked to the material, carried throughout the presentation, and true to your personality.

HAVE VIVID SUPPORTING MATERIAL

Briefings can get bogged down with statistics and facts. To help your audience make sense of the information and retain it, incorporate interesting supporting material. Make a statistic come alive by telling a story about a person the audience can relate to that exemplifies the statistic. Explain esoteric information with a metaphor or analogy that allows listeners to understand something new in terms of something they already know. (See chapter 16 for more on supporting material.) Pictures, graphs, props, and other audio/visual aids can also enhance learning. Research shows that we retain more when we hear and see something, so a few carefully selected presentation aids will help listeners better understand and remember your message. (See chapter 21 for more on presentation aids.)

INVOLVE THE AUDIENCE

Another way to prevent eyes from glazing over during your informative speech is by engaging participants. Not every suggestion below will work for every speech—breaking out into small groups to discuss the application of a concept works for a training program but would be bizarre in a client briefing.

Here is a broad list of ideas to consider using when you want to involve your audience:

- Pointed rhetorical questions to get your audience thinking.

- Actual questions that solicit input from attendees.

- Tell audience to imagine something so they see it in their mind's eye.

- Give a quiz. Have listeners raise hands for their answer or hold up a colored piece of paper you provided them to indicate their response. Written self-assessments also can be a useful tool during training programs.

- Conduct a Q&A session. Consider inviting questions by providing pen and paper or taking them via Twitter, Facebook, or other social media so people who aren't comfortable speaking up can participate too. Think about opening your speech with Q&A or taking questions at the end of each main section when conducting a long briefing or training.

- Use stories. Narratives are inherently participatory because listeners put themselves in stories they hear and make comparisons to their own experiences. Consider including, with permission, firsthand experiences of audience members that you collected beforehand.

- Call and response. This is helpful when you have covered several key points in a training session or how-to speech and want participants to repeat them back to you to aid retention.

Don't poison your listeners with boredom. Prevent eyes from glazing over by following these tips when you give informative speeches.

EXERCISE

Using the Sandwich Structure, craft and deliver a three to four minute presentation on a hobby or personal interest. Consider using a prop, such as actual objects or photographs, to help explain your topic.

ACTIVITY

Watch Joe Smith's TED Talk entitled, "How to Use a Paper Towel" (www.ted.com/talks/joe_smith_how_to_use_a_paper_towel). What was his take-away message? Was it easy to identify and remember? Why? What techniques were used to engage audience members and help them retain information? What could Smith have done to make his presentation more effective? ▪

—————— CHAPTER 24 ——————

WHERE YOU SAY IT
Training Programs and Lectures

Do you remember your favorite teacher? Chances are your favorite teacher didn't just stand in front of a classroom and lecture, but managed to get you involved in the material you were learning.

Many professionals do not consider themselves teachers by trade. But as their areas of expertise develop, they surely will be called upon to educate others. Such opportunities may come by way of training programs for colleagues, members of a professional association, or participants at an industry conference. Or they may present as opportunities to teach learners at a community center, or students at a local school, college, or university.

Here are some tips to make the most of your next opportunity to train or teach an audience:

CAREFULLY CRAFT LEARNING OUTCOMES

In most presentations, speakers give an overview of the main ideas they will cover. But in a training program, make sure you give that overview by way of specific learning outcomes. The outcomes tell participants what whey will be able to do after your session.

Encourage active learning by crafting outcomes that start with verbs like: create, solve, plan, design, assess, justify, prove, and apply. You can include some verbs that get at lower-order thinking skills, such as identify, classify, list, describe, compare, and report, but they should not make up the bulk of learning objectives for a training session.

SHIFT THE FOCUS TO DOING

Pedagogical methods long have centered on lecturing students—telling them what the instructor knows. It calls to mind the boring professor who talks to the chalkboard while students struggle to stay awake.

CURRENT RESEARCH IN PEDAGOGY ENCOURAGES ACTIVE LEARNING OVER PASSIVE LEARNING.

More recently, there was a shift to demonstration—showing students what the instructor is talking about. Advances in technology since the 1990's have made it easier to incorporate multimedia into lectures. No doubt, seeing and listening is more engaging and improves recall compared to listening alone, but it still encourages passive learning.

Current research in pedagogy encourages active learning over passive learning—having students do something rather than just telling and/or showing them how to do it. Rather than focusing on lower-order thinking skills from Bloom's Taxonomy, like reciting and classifying, teachers and trainers should engage students in higher-order thinking skills, like analyzing and evaluating. Learner retention skyrockets when teachers go beyond telling and showing, and get students discussing, practicing, and ultimately, teaching others.

PROVIDE ACTIVE LEARNING OPPORTUNITIES

One reason that many teachers stick to telling and showing is that they feel compelled to "cover all the material." But if listeners aren't retaining what you're teaching, it makes sense to cover less material and to provide more opportunities for active learning and retention.

There are many ways to promote active learning, but here four ideas to help get you started.

IN-CLASS QUIZZES

Have students respond to questions about a reading or other material by raising a hand or holding up a card (could be a T and F for true or false questions, or a colored card that corresponds to answer A, B, C, etc.). Use responses to gauge understanding and to start a discussion by asking students who responded with a correct answer to explain it.

CHECK FOR UNDERSTANDING

At points of transition in training sessions or lectures, ask participants what they learned. You will aid memory by having them describe concepts in their own words and will reinforce those ideas for other audience members. You also will identify any gaps in learning or misunderstandings that you may need to clear up.

THINK, PAIR, SHARE

Pose a question, observation, or prompt and ask students to think about it for a few moments. Then, have individuals work with a neighbor or in a small group to discuss their answers. Finally, ask pairs or groups to share responses and to start a class discussion on the issues raised. This can be done with lower-order thinking skills, but is particularly effective when used with scenarios, case studies, role-playing, and other prompts that foster high-order thinking skills.

DEBATE

Assign listeners to support or oppose an issue. Have each team craft several arguments for the position, support each argument with evidence, and prepare rebuttals to likely objections from the other team. Time the presenters for each argument; then allow questions from the opposing team. Foster back-and-forth discussion and rebuttals from students who did not formally present an argument.

For additional active-learning activities, check out this guide: http://activelearning.uta.edu/facstaff/ALtechniques.htm

Hopefully this chapter spurred you to think of your favorite teacher and the powerful impact he or she had on your life. May it serve as motivation to seek out opportunities to share your expertise with others. Think of those training and teaching opportunities not as a platform to tell and show what you know, but as a way to guide learners as they understand, clarify, apply, analyze, judge, and reflect on material you share with them.

EXERCISE

Using the Sandwich Structure, craft and deliver a three to four minute how-to speech. Select a topic based on your personal interests or professional expertise, but make sure to make your subject relevant and useful to listeners. Demonstrate your topic using gestures and body movements, or with a presentation aid such as a photograph, diagram, video, or prop.

ACTIVITY

Attend a class, workshop, or lecture and evaluate the instructor. What were the learning outcomes for the session? Were they clearly articulated? What active learning techniques were employed? Did the instructor focus on telling and showing students? Or did he or she have learners do something? What could the instructor have done differently to make the program more engaging and to increase understanding? ▪

—————— CHAPTER 25 ——————

WHERE YOU SAY IT
Persuasive Speeches and Pitches

Billy Mays. You might recognize the name. You probably recognize the voice. Mays was a fixture of late-night infomercials during the late 1990's and early 2000's. With his signature high-energy voice, Mays was the pitchman for a variety of products: OxyClean, Snuggies, and the Big City Slider Station, to name just a few. No matter what the product was, you knew that Billy was trying to sell it.

Mays was an over-the-top example of a salesman. But when you think about it, all professionals are salespeople—they may be selling themselves for a new job or promotion, selling colleagues on a new business strategy, or pitching a product or service to prospective clients. And the ability to sway an audience is crucial to success in our personal lives as well (think of situations like convincing someone to go on a date, negotiating a good deal on a new car, or persuading a neighbor to turn down his or her music at night so you can sleep).

Because persuasion is both a common and crucial presentation skill, this chapter will explore three useful ways of thinking about persuasion and will point out how you can apply them to your next attempt to influence someone.

ARISTOTLE

Long before the days of infomercials, ancient Greeks (and later Romans) were interested in the study of persuasion. It was the cornerstone of classical education, which stands to reason. For example, in Athens during the 5th Century BCE, if you were a male over 18 and free (i.e., not a slave), you were expected to represent yourself in legal matters, legislative debates, as well as in ceremonial settings like funerals. You wouldn't have had attorneys, lawmakers, and clergy to speak on your behalf.

One of the most celebrated treatises on persuasion is Aristotle's *Rhetoric*, which dates to the 4th Century BCE. In it, he defined rhetoric as "The faculty of observing, in any given case, the available means of persuasion."[1] Aristotle went on to classify those available means of persuasion, focusing mainly on the three types of appeals that a speaker can make: ethos, pathos, and logos.

Appeals to ethos are ones that bolster the speaker's credibility—his or her goodwill, good sense, and good moral character. Pathos refers to appeals to emotion, when a speaker invites an audience to feel and imagine what he or she has experienced. And logos has to do with reasoning, specifically the structure and content of an argument.

Takeaway

Present-day speakers are well served to use Aristotle's classical concepts of ethos, pathos, and logos to craft balanced appeals in their persuasive pitches. All too often, presenters rely on facts, figures, and data (heavy on logos). They often ignore ethos and pathos, appeals that often can be made by telling stories. See chapter 17 for more on using stories as supporting material.

MONROE

Fast forward from antiquity to the 1930's when Alan Monroe, a professor at Purdue University, coined a structure for persuasive speeches. Called

Monroe's Motivated Sequence, the core elements are, in order: attention, need, satisfaction, visualization, and action.[2]

1. ATTENTION

Effectively persuading listeners requires speakers to garner the attention of audience members at the outset of the presentation. (See chapter 20 for more on attention getting devices.) You are about to ask audience members to change their minds or their behavior. If they are not engaged in the presentation from the beginning, it is highly unlikely you will sway them.

2. NEED

After you get the attention of the audience, the second element of persuasion is establishing a need. You, as a presenter, need to demonstrate that there is a problem, gap, injustice, or some other deficiency that exists in the world today.

Why is this step necessary? Well, imagine if you took your car to the shop for an oil change. The mechanic asks if you want to buy an additional service for $100. Naturally, you would ask, "Do I need it?" If he or she responds, "No, it's just a really cool new product," are you going to buy it? Probably not. The repair person must show you the need for the service. What problem does it fix? What calamity does it prevent? Without a clear and immediate need, it isn't likely that you will pay up.

3. SATISFACTION

Now, you have the attention of listeners and you have demonstrated that a need exists and requires action. But how can the need be satisfied? What is your proposed solution to the problem you identified? That is the next element of persuasive structure, as defined in Monroe's Motivated Sequence.

In demonstrating how a need can be satisfied, there are a few things to consider. Most importantly, make sure that you actually address how the need is satisfied. That may seem obvious, but you would be surprised how many people construct doomsday scenarios and then offer the most inconsequential plans to satisfy that need.

In addition, provide enough detail to make the audience feel comfortable that you have thought through how the need can be satisfied. You might give examples of similar solutions that have worked elsewhere. Also, make a point of showing that your solution is within the realm of the feasible. That's not to say that you shouldn't propose revolutionary ideas or think outside the box. But, if your mechanic's idea for fixing a worn-out set of brake pads is to buy a new sports car, he or she won't be taken seriously.

4. VISUALIZATION

Visualization is the process of helping your audience imagine the benefits that will come after the need is satisfied. This involves painting a picture of what the world will look like to the audience member with the solution enacted.

If you are selling additional services at an auto repair shop, you might discuss extra benefits (depending on the service) such as increased safety or fuel mileage, or decreased maintenance costs or emissions. You are helping your listener see how the satisfaction step will benefit him or her. Remember audience members don't care how the plan benefits the speaker (e.g., knowing the mechanic will have a higher profit margin by selling a new product is not convincing at all). Put yourself in the shoes of the listener when crafting the visualization step.

5. ACTION

The final step in Monroe's Motivated Sequence is telling audience members what specifically they can do to enact the solution. The action step should be tailored to the audience and should seem somewhat easy to accomplish. For the mechanic selling a product, the action step could include when, where, and how the customer could purchase it. If you are strengthening or weakening the bond between listeners and a position, then the action step might be a statement of what they need to remember or take away from your presentation. If you are advocating a change in policy, the action step may be signing an online petition or contacting one's representative in a legislative body.

These five steps can be organized as the main points of a presentation, or they can be used within each main point (see sidebar). Depending on the context and knowledge base of audience members, some elements might need more elaboration, some less. But, in the end, persuasion is like a chain, you need each link in the chain to be strong in order for the chain to do its job.

AUDIENCE MEMBERS YOU ARE HOPING TO PERSUADE WANT TO KNOW, "WHAT'S IN IT FOR ME?" AN INSTINCT FOR SELF-PRESERVATION LIES DEEP WITHIN EVERYONE.

Takeaway

Persuasive speakers can use the five steps of Monroe's Motivated Sequence to structure their thoughts in a range of speaking situations—from a formal presentation to a casual conversation. They should also remember the importance of thinking of a proposal's benefits in terms of the listener (not themselves). Audience members you are hoping to persuade want to know, "What's in it for me?" An instinct for self-preservation lies deep within everyone; people care first and foremost about themselves. Accordingly, if you want to land a new job, don't focus on how much you will learn and grow professionally in the position. Tell the person hiring you how you will give them peace of mind, make his or her life easier, provide creative solutions to problems, or even make him or her look good to higher ups.

THE CONVERSION MYTH

When people casually use the term *persuasion*, they often are referring to wholesale change. For example, if you are trying to convince your boss to let you leave work a few hours early on the Friday of a holiday weekend, your boss might say, "Alright, you've persuaded me. You can leave early." In this sense, you have converted your boss from one opinion to another. Conversion is certainly one possible persuasive purpose. What, then, is meant by the Conversion Myth?

The Conversion Myth refers to the common and mistaken belief that the sole purpose of persuasion is to convert a person from one belief to another. In fact, conversion is just one persuasive purpose. But there are others, and it is important to remember that a persuasive presentation can be successful even if it is not intended to change the attitudes or actions of listeners.

THE CONVERSION MYTH REFERS TO THE COMMON AND MISTAKEN BELIEF THAT THE SOLE PURPOSE OF PERSUASION IS TO CONVERT A PERSON FROM ONE BELIEF TO ANOTHER.

Other than conversion, a presenter may seek to *strengthen the bond* between the audience and an idea or behavior. At political campaign rallies, for example, the audience is composed of supporters of a candidate. When the candidate speaks, they are trying to pump up the crowd. The candidate probably will remind the audience of the values he or she stands for, as well as discuss what is at stake in the election. Audience members who already share your views or already behave the way that you are asking them to behave can be persuaded to become more committed to that view or behavior.

Another persuasive purpose can be to *weaken the bond* between an audience and their ideas or behaviors. Imagine that you start a widget company. This is a widget that most offices already have, but your version of this widget is better. You make an appointment to present your widget to the person in charge of purchasing. Ideally, you want to present you widget and have the decision maker say, "Great! You've got our business." But, in general, humans are resistant to change. So, if you cannot get their business at that moment, you at least want

Here is a sample structure in which the motivational sequence serves as the main points for the presentation:

I. Introduction
    A. AGD [Attention Step]
    B. Orienting Material
    C. Thesis/Controlling Idea
    D. Preview
II. Problem [Need Step]
    A. Problem 1
        1. Supporting Material
    B. Problem 2
        1. Supporting Material
III. Solution [Satisfaction Step]
    A. Details about the solution
    B. More details
    C. More details
IV. Advantages [Visualization Step]
    A. Advantage 1
    B. Advantage 2
V. Conclusion [Action Step]
    A. Review main points
    B. Restate thesis
    C. Call to action
    D. Clinch

Here is a sample structure in which the motivational structure is incorporated within a topical pattern of arrangement:

I. Introduction
    A. AGD [Attention Step]
    B. Orienting Material
    C. Thesis/Controlling Idea
    D. Preview
II. Topic 1
    A. Need 1
        1. Supporting Material
    B. Satisfaction 1
        1. Supporting Material
    C. Visualization 1
        1. Supporting Material
III. Topic 2
    A. Need 2
        1. Supporting Material
    B. Satisfaction 2
        1. Supporting Material
    C. Visualization 2
        1. Supporting Material
V. Conclusion [Action Step]
    A. Review main points
    B. Restate thesis
    C. Call to action
    D. Clinch

to deliver a presentation that shows the benefits of your widget and establishes your character. This might weaken the bond between the decision maker and their commitment to your competitor. In weakening that bond, you've created a potential opening for the future.

Lastly, a presenter's purpose might be to *encourage a specific action*. Encouraging action may contain elements of conversion, strengthening a bond, or weakening a bond. What makes this persuasive purpose distinct is that you are asking the audience to do something. Here we can return to Billy Mays. He is not asking that we think differently about the products we buy. Rather, he is asking his audience to pick up the phone or log onto a website to take action and buy the product. In some ways, this can be the most difficult persuasive purpose because you are asking the audience to give up a scarce resource—time or money. Encouraging a specific action can be difficult, which is why understanding persuasive structure is important.

Ultimately, as a presenter you need to do a thorough analysis of your audience and situation to determine an appropriate persuasive message. (See chapter 12 for details on audience analysis.) In many instances, arguing for wholesale change may involve asking listeners to go further than they are ready or willing to go. And doing so could have the opposite impact, known as the Boomerang Effect,[3] of making listeners resistant to your proposal. The persuasive process often is incremental and lengthy. Remember that aiming to strengthen bonds or to weaken bonds are both legitimate persuasive purposes.

EXERCISE

In a class or workshop setting, have each participant contribute one dollar to a collection of money. With the dollar, each person has "bought" one minute of speaking time. During a one-minute pitch, each speaker must use Monroe's Motivated Sequence to convince listeners to vote for his or her unique plan for spending the pot of money. Allow participants to vote for two or three distinct proposals after all the pitches are given. Give the pot of money to the highest vote earners (or split the pot if there is a tie). Why did the winning pitch earn the most votes? What does it say about audience members and their motivation for accepting persuasive claims?

ACTIVITY

Watch a significant and contemporary persuasive speech (for a comprehensive list of contemporary presidential speeches, go to www.presidentialrhetoric.com). Identify the appeals the speaker made to ethos, pathos, and logos. Which appeals were most persuasive to you? Why? Was there balance in the use of the three types of persuasive appeals? What appeals could the speaker have eliminated or added to make his or her speech more compelling? ∎

1. Aristotle. *Rhetoric*. Trans. W. Rhys. Roberts. Ed. W.D. Ross. Cosimo Press, 2010. Print. 6.

2. Monroe, Alan H. *Principles and Types of Speech*. Glenview, IL: Scott Foresman, 1935. Print. This is the first edition. The book has had many editions with various authors.

3. Hoveland, Carl Iver, Irving Lester Janis, and Harold H. Kelley. *Communication and Persuasion: Psychology Studies of Opinion Change*. New Haven, CT: Yale University Press, 1954. Print.

———— CHAPTER 26 ————

WHERE YOU SAY IT
Meetings

Meetings—some are productive, others are painful. Apply principles of preparing and delivering effective presentations and your colleagues won't cringe when they get an invitation to your meeting. The following suggestions pertain to preparing the content of your meeting:

MAKE SURE IT'S WORTH DOING

Savvy speakers know that not every invitation to speak is worth accepting. Similarly, determine whether you need to hold a meeting to reach your objective. If you want to brainstorm ideas or collaborate on a solution to a problem, assembling a group of people makes sense. But if you are informing people on a new policy or otherwise engaging in one-way communication, consider sending a memorandum or providing an online tutorial instead.

RESEARCH YOUR AUDIENCE

Just as you should research your audience before crafting a presentation, research the people who will be participating in your meeting—and only include people who really need to be there. If you don't already know expected participants, find out about their background and issues of interest from their company biography, LinkedIn profile, media reports, and even information you can glean from trusted friends and colleagues. When you do know expected participants, take time to find out what they want to discuss, what their perspective is on issues being discussed, and what they plan to say if asked to report on a related project.

When possible or appropriate, it is best to find out about dissent or problems before the meeting, so you can take action or, at the very least, be prepared to address such issues during the meeting. As a presenter, you never want to be caught flat-footed. The fewer surprises, the smoother your meeting will run.

Also, find out the best time and place for participants to meet. Try to accommodate schedules and preferences. And remember that nobody wants to be at a meeting at 4:00 p.m. on a Friday afternoon. After details are set, send a meeting invite with details—subject, time, location, agenda, etc. And a reminder e-mail is in order if you schedule your meeting more than a few days in advance.

HAVE A THESIS

Like a speech, a meeting needs a general purpose and thesis. Do you want to brainstorm? Make a decision? Get status updates? On what specific topic? Make sure the purpose is clear and the goal is limited enough in scope that the objective can be met in the time allotted. Keep the meeting time reasonable— expectations vary from industry to industry, but 30 to 90 minutes will help ensure participants stay engaged. Schedule the shortest possible meeting to achieve your objective and make sure all participants know the general purpose and thesis of the meeting beforehand.

PREPARE AN OUTLINE

Presentations usually have two or three main points that support the thesis. So too should a meeting. Prepare an outline to identify the main issues you will discuss and decide how much time you will devote to each issue. If meeting participants are reporting on issues you identify—a great way to increase involvement—make sure to let them know in advance, including how long they will have for their contribution.

The outline of your meeting should be put in writing. That's your agenda. It should be settled with meeting participants ahead of time, when appropriate, and distributed in advance. Bring copies of the agenda to the meeting for all participants. Include what time you will move to each agenda item to avoid a meeting that runs late.

PRACTICE

If you want to come across as confident, polished, and professional, rehearse. You do it when you deliver a presentation and should too for your speaking parts in a meeting. Just because you're sitting down or speaking to a small group doesn't mean you can or should wing it. After all, the stakes can be particularly high at intimate meetings—like performance evaluations and client pitches.

If possible, practice six times for success; that's when the material will stick and you won't struggle to remember what you want to say next or stumble over the wording of what you say. It's when you will be polished and professional. (See chapter 22 for more on rehearsals.)

DELIVERY

Just as there are many parallels between planning a meeting and crafting a presentation, speakers are well served to apply principles of effective speech delivery when conducting meetings. The following suggestions pertain to delivering the content of your meeting:

COMMAND THE ROOM

The leader of a meeting must take control. When approaching the lectern, a confident speaker has great posture; moves slowly and purposefully; smiles; makes eye contact with members of the audience; starts with a loud, clear voice; and, opens with a carefully crafted and articulate introduction rather than junk words like "um" or "so." With the exception of walking to the head of a table versus a lectern, it is no different for kicking off a meeting.

Your command of the room must continue throughout the meeting. If a participant is straying from the topic at hand, speaking too long or dominating the conversation, it is your responsibility to politely but firmly interrupt to get the meeting back on track or to include other attendees.

START STRONG AND ON TIME

Always hook your audience with a catchy opening when giving a speech. When leading a meeting, make sure to open with something light and positive. Different leaders will open in different ways, depending on their personality, leadership style, and type of meeting they are running. Some ideas for openings are: giving out an award, recognizing a professional or personal achievement of a participant, sharing a topical and inspirational quotation, or telling a humorous and relevant story. Meetings should be efficient, but they shouldn't be impersonal. Make an effort to establish rapport or build a team. Find techniques to do this that work for the context of your meeting and your leadership style.

Whatever you do to open a meeting, do it on time. Starting late suggests that the meeting is disorganized or that the agenda will not be followed closely. Even if key players are not present, start. If you don't, they will continue to come late and waste the time of everyone else involved. If you do start on time, latecomers will get the message.

INTRODUCTORY MATERIAL

Great speeches have some set-up after the catchy opening sentence and so too should a meeting. After you open, make sure to state the purpose of the meeting so everyone is on the same page, even if participants didn't review the agenda in advance.

Consider a brief round of introductions if participants don't already know one another. Some people are bad with names even after a few meetings, so err on the side of caution when deciding whether to review names.

SIGNPOST

The adage, "Tell them what you're going to tell them; tell them; tell them what you told them," holds true for presentations as well as meetings. Give participant signposts, or a roadmap of how the meeting will unfold. After the opening and introductory material, preview the agenda, including issues that will be discussed and how the meeting will be structured. Though this information is on the agenda, it should be said aloud too.

When meetings are contentious or participants are known to derail the agenda, it is especially important to set out clear expectation as to who will speak, how participants will be recognized, what they will talk about, how long they can speak, and how they will be interrupted if they go over or stray from the subject at hand.

WHEN MEETINGS ARE CONTENTIOUS OR PARTICIPANTS ARE KNOWN TO DERAIL THE AGENDA, IT IS ESPECIALLY IMPORTANT TO SET OUT CLEAR EXPECTATIONS.

Have a clear transition from one issue to the next. If a participant is talking too long or getting off topic, follow through with your promise to interrupt and get the meeting back on track. It isn't rude when you've laid out expectations and hold all participants to the same standards. On the contrary, failing to interrupt would be rude to other participants who were promised a meeting on certain issues in a certain timeframe.

To interrupt, wait until the speaker is finishing a sentence or taking a breath (and believe it not, every speaker will breathe at some point). Then, pleasantly say, "Morgan, thank you for bringing up that important issue. It's not on our agenda today, so after the meeting, I'll be in touch with you to set a time for the two of us to discuss it further. Right now, it's time to move on to the third item on today's agenda."

Finally, as you review what happened at the meeting, recap for each agenda item the steps participants decided to take, noting who will take the lead as well as how and when he or she will report back.

WRAP UP AND END ON TIME

You gain goodwill by ending a presentation a few minutes early. Similarly, try to end your meeting a little early and never late. Meeting participants respect leaders who respect their time. Don't forget to thank participants. If another meeting is scheduled or needs to be scheduled, confirm a time and location, if possible. If your meeting is part of a larger program or conference, tell attendees what is coming next and where to go. It never hurts to follow up in writing with a recap of your thank yous and action items.

Apply the best practices of crafting and delivering effective presentations to ensure your meetings will be productive and that attendees will gladly accept your next meeting invitation.

EXERCISE

When attending a meeting, we often focus on the content but underappreciate how that content was delivered. The next time you find yourself in a meeting, ask yourself the following questions about the delivery style of the leader and other speakers: What communicative behaviors help the meeting run smoothly? Which ones hinder the flow of the meeting? Which ones establish authority of the speaker? Which undermine it? How did the leader/facilitator manage difficult moments or personalities in the meeting?

ACTIVITY

Identify a scenario in which a meeting is necessary. There should be a professional context (the type of business or organization), an impetus for the meeting (a crisis, a quarterly sales meeting, preparation for a year-end review, etc.), and an objective that the group is working toward (making a decision, brainstorming ideas, etc.).

On strips of paper, write down the "characters" that you see in meetings. These can be the interrupter, the one-word answerer, the jokester, the person who keeps people on track, the interpreter (i.e., the person who takes the ramblings of one member or the group and makes a coherent statement from it), etc. Half of the strips should be positive behaviors and half should be negative (or at least complicated) behaviors. One of the strips should say "facilitator."

Gather a group of collaborators, and assign roles written on the strips of paper to each of the meeting participants. Run the mock meeting, improvising details where necessary, with each participant performing their assigned behavior. All participants should attempt to engage the meeting in good faith. At the end, discuss the following questions: What strategies were effective for dealing with the positive and negative behaviors during the meeting? What didn't work? Why? How could the situation have been handled differently?

Reflect on your communication behaviors during meetings when you aren't assigned a role. What role(s) do you play in various meeting contexts? How might this help or hinder your perceived abilities as a team player or as a leader? What might you do differently in specific meeting contexts to be more effective in the future? ▪

---------- CHAPTER 27 ----------

WHERE YOU SAY IT
Teleconferences, Videoconferences, and Webinars

Now that smartphones and computers are commonplace, and the global economy is increasingly interconnected, it is no wonder that more and more workplace communication takes place via the phone or the computer. That's why this chapter is dedicated to offering specific tips for speaking effectively during teleconferences, videoconferences, and webinars.

Remember, you will find useful tips in other chapters to help you prepare content for specific types of presentations that may take place using these various media, such as meetings (see chapter 26), job interviews (see chapter 31), and training programs (see chapter 24). Just because you aren't physically in the same room as the people you are speaking to, doesn't mean that you should wing the content of your presentation.

TELECONFERENCES

Teleconferences occur when you are meeting with one or more people by phone. The fact that meeting participants cannot see one another can lead to a lack of professionalism that makes this mode of communication less effective. Ensure your telephone speaking skills match your in-person speaking skills by following these simple guidelines:

FIND A SUITABLE WORKSPACE

If you are dialing into a teleconference, there's always the temptation to do it from the road. And while it might be nice to squeeze in a meeting via phone while you are running errands, there is no way you can be as focused when dialing in from your car (moving or parked) or a coffee shop.

Then, there's the problem of distractions—honking from the vehicle you just accidentally cut off or from the server yelling out an order in a café. Even if you could stay focused in this environment (and it is not likely you would), others on the call will be distracted by the background racket and might infer that you are not serious about the meeting.

WEAR APPROPRIATE CLOTHES DURING TELECONFERENCES, EVEN THOUGH PEOPLE ON THE OTHER END OF THE LINE CAN'T SEE YOU.

Make sure that you find a private and quiet place to call in. If you are at home, turn off televisions, radios, and other gadgets that might cause a distraction; and if you work in an open office, try to book a small conference room to conduct important meetings by phone. Aim to use a landline telephone whenever possible to improve call quality.

DRESS PROFESSIONALLY

Wear work appropriate clothes during teleconferences, even though people on the other end of the line can't see you. If you are calling in from home or from an office with a very casual atmosphere, still dress to impress. After all, speakers preform at their peak when they feel their best. It is difficult to exude confidence in pajamas or ratty jeans.

STAND UP

In the same vein as dressing professionally, you also should stand up to speak during teleconferences. Use a headset so you can have the tall, confident posture you would use during an in-person presentation and so that you can gesture broadly and purposefully while you speak. (See chapter 4 for more on effective stance.)

When you are speaking from a standing position, you will be more likely to project your voice, to speak with enthusiasm, and to be polished (avoiding junk words and expressing your ideas more concisely). Speakers are more likely to slip into a more casual speaking styles and poor speaking habits if they are sitting down in a comfortable space and wearing street clothes.

ENUMERATE YOUR POINTS

Interruptions can be a problem during teleconferences. Others you are meeting with can't see your body language—a key way that presenters signal that they are almost done speaking or are ready to have a turn in the conversation during face-to-face conversations. To combat interruptions, number your points when you are responding. For example, you could say, "There are three reasons why we should pursue this course of action. First . . . " This provides a preview that gives everyone a sense of how long you are speaking and provides a means of overriding an attempt at an interruption. Instead, you might say, "Let me quickly finish the third reason before we move on to discuss your concerns." But, it requires you to be concise with your points. Participants in your teleconference will have limited patience if you tend to filibuster.

REPEAT YOUR NAME

When you are speaking to several people, people who don't know you well, or to a large group on a teleconference, be sure to re-introduce yourself briefly each time you offer a response. It need not be lengthy—"This is Taylor here responding to Jim's concern about the project timeline." Such an introduction ensures participants know who is talking and can prevent misunderstandings or confusion.

VIDEOCONFERENCES

Whether you use Skype, FaceTime, or another video-calling service, here are a few tips that will improve your effectiveness in this particular type of computer-mediated communication.

TEST YOUR TECHNOLOGY

As is the case with PowerPoint and other presentation software, Murphy's Law seemingly holds true for videoconference calls as well: If something can go wrong with the technology, it will. Try to prevent technological difficulties by testing and re-testing the technology you are using. Also prepare a back-up plan in case it does fail. For example, you might want to have a call-in number and code ready to go for a teleconference in case your videoconference is a bust. Lastly, consider using a headset or some other audio capture device aside from your computer's microphone. Using something that better captures your voice while eliminating echoes or ambient sounds will increase the professional quality of you presentation.

TAKE A WIDE ANGLE

Many speakers zoom their webcam in too tight for videoconferences (likely because they use the webcam on their computer and sit too close to it). This leads to the phenomenon of the talking head—everyone on the videoconference sees just the speaker's head, which can make the speaker appear awkward or even silly.

Prevent this problem by taking a wider camera angle. Zoom out so that the webcam is capturing your head, neck, shoulders, and even your upper body from the waist up. This is a more flattering view and can provide listeners the opportunity to see hand gestures and other non-verbal cues. Of course, such a setup will mean that you can't easily reference notes on your computer screen; plan ahead and print out any materials that you will need to refer to during the course of the videoconference.

CREATE A PROFESSIONAL BACKDROP

When you take a wider angle, remember that fellow participants on the videoconference call can now see more of the room from which you are speaking. If you have the take-out box from lunch and a messy stack of papers in the screenshot, you look unpolished before you even say a word.

It doesn't take much effort to create a professional backdrop for your videoconference. A tidy bookcase behind an office chair or a small table with flowers next to an armchair that you are sitting in will do the trick. Just check the lighting (avoid sitting right in front of a window, for example) and try not to situate yourself directly in the center of the shot (being a little off center adds visual interest).

WEBINARS

When you lead a workshop or seminar online, you are conducting a webinar. And while it is important to follow best practices of training programs (see chapter 24 for more), you also can boost your effectiveness in this online form of communication by keeping a few suggestions in mind.

For webinars that are delivered live (also known as synchronous), remember to:

SET-UP EARLY AND START ON TIME

Plan to have ample time to troubleshoot any technological problems before the start of your live webinar. As participants start joining, make several announcements to welcome them and let them know when the program will get underway; you don't want listeners to wait too long without acknowledgement. Then, start at the appointed time so you don't waste the time of audience members. You might make your introduction a little long to account for latecomers, but do begin on time.

WELCOME PARTICIPANTS SEVERAL TIMES

After the webinar is underway, continue to welcome new participants during the first five to seven minutes of the program. Don't scold latecomers; welcome them warmly and get them up to speed by saying something brief, such as, "If you are just joining us, thanks for participating in the Acme webinar on XYZ topic. If you'd like to ask a question, please type it into the box on the bottom right of your screen and then click the submit button."

REMIND LISTENERS HOW TO INTERACT

As the last example showed, you should tell participants how to interact. Most live webinar hosting services have tools for participants to ask questions. At the beginning of the program, at the end of each segment, and at the end of the program, remind listeners how to pose a question. Plan time at the end of each major segment and the end of the program to field questions and keep the webinar interactive.

Based on your webinar hosting service, you may also have other interactive tools at your disposal, such as a quick poll (where participants answer a live multiple-choice question posed by the leader of the webinar) or online discussion (where participants can interact online by responding to topics raised by the webinar leader as well as to comments written by other participants). Research and test different options beforehand; include a few into the outline of the content of your webinar, making sure you allot enough time to conduct them during the program.

LIMIT IT TO ONE HOUR

Depending on the audience, interactive and in-person training programs can run as long as 90 minutes to two hours without a break. But webinars, even synchronous and interactive ones, are best limited to one hour. It is that much harder over a computer-mediated format to maintain the attention of listeners (especially over online distractions like e-mail, Facebook, and Twitter). To cover your material in a 60-minute timeframe, make sure you narrow your topic; it is better to go in depth on a narrow topic than to give a surface-level understanding of a broad one.

And for webinars that are pre-recorded (also known as asynchronous), it is a good idea to:

KEEP SEGMENTS SHORT

If it is difficult to maintain the attention of participants during a live workshop, imagine how much harder it is during a pre-recorded webinar. To prevent listeners from turning out or signing off, organize your webinar in a series of short segments—ideally about five to 10 minutes each. You can have an hour or even more of material total, but break it into easily digestible pieces that participants can move through at their own pace.

INCLUDE INTERACTIVE ELEMENTS

Consider including an activity or exercise that participants can do at the end of each segment to reinforce new principles or practice new skills. You might even make the webinar a hybrid between recorded (asynchronous) and live (synchronous) by scheduling live online discussions or Q&A sessions at a certain points in the program that participants can otherwise move through independently.

BE ESPECIALLY CLEAR

Of course, being clear relates to the quality of the video and audio of your presentation. Once you have figured out the technology and setup for your presentation, you can focus on achieving clarity in the content.

It is always important to strive for clarity in the structure, descriptions, explanations, and directions you provide during presentations. But this need is magnified in the case of recorded webinars because listeners can't ask for immediate clarification if they don't understand something.

To highlight the structure of your material, provide overt objectives as well as signposting (the preview, review, and transitions between points). For descriptions and explanations, consider using a mix of analogies, metaphors, visual aids, and quotations to make your point. And to clarify directions, consider supplementing verbal instructions with written bullet points so participants can hear and see each step.

There is no doubt that technological advancement will bring new opportunities to connect with clients and colleagues by phone and computer. Make sure you shine in these speaking situations by preparing your content appropriately (for a meeting, job interview, training program, etc.), and also by following best practices of communicating via a teleconference, a videoconference, or a webinar.

EXERCISE

Prepare a three to four minute how-to speech. Deliver it to a listener or group of listeners once by phone, once by Skype or FaceTime, and once with a video recording by YouTube or another video sharing or webinar service. What were the advantages and disadvantages of presenting your speech in each of these three formats? How could you have changed your presentation to make your speech more effective in each format? Which mediated format did listeners prefer? Why?

ACTIVITY

Ask a friend, classmate, or colleague to Skype or FaceTime with you. Change the backdrop, lighting, computer location, chair location, etc. and ask your collaborator which elements they preferred and why. Also ask about the quality of the sound and picture in various configurations so you will know what will work best for future videoconferences. ∎

—————— CHAPTER 28 ——————

WHERE YOU SAY IT
Panel Moderation and Group Presentations

"A great panel moderator is like a great party host: making everyone feel welcome, knowing how to avoid or handle lulls, knowing how to get a conversation going between others, knowing how to rescue someone from an inappropriate or overly long conversation, and knowing how to wrap things up when it's time for the party to end—all done with alertness and diplomacy, and without expecting to be the center of attention," explained Jim Becker, an information technology director who spent years moderating panels as well as planning meetings and conferences.

Just like a great party requires careful preparation, so does a great panel or group presentation. Here is what a moderator/facilitator can do beforehand to ensure that guests—speakers and the audience—have a positive experience:

ANALYZE THE AUDIENCE

When preparing a panel, the moderator and/or conference planner should identify the target audience. Ideally, research should be conducted via questionnaires and interviews to learn about the needs and interests of audience members. (See chapter 12 for more on analyzing the situation and audience.) Aim to put on a panel addressing a timely issue that falls at the intersection of what listeners care about and what presenters know about.

SELECT PARTICIPANTS

Along with the right topic, select the right panelists to ensure a packed event. Invite thought leaders and newsmakers who have credibility on the issue, as well as an important point of view. Aim to showcase a range of perspectives.

Seek out panelists who are dynamic speakers; the best authorities on a topic don't always make the best panelists. Similarly, select speakers who are willing to present within the parameters (topic, time constraints, etc.) of the panel. Some high-profile speakers have a stump speech and won't tailor their presentation for specific audiences and situations. Find someone who will.

Aim high. When you identify the perfect presenter for your panel, extend an invitation. No one can say "yes" if you don't ask.

Recruit one or two extra panelists to account for cancellations. Each industry and conference differs, but most panels have three to five panelists. Strive for balance between breadth and depth—have a range of perspectives and enough time for a thorough discussion. Include sufficient time for questions from audience members, as well as answers from and exchanges between panelists.

CONFIRM AND RECONFIRM

After panelists accept, confirm the when and where in writing. Also explain your vision for the panel: what it is about, why panelists are on it, what they should address to avoid repetition, how long they should speak, how the panel will unfold, how question and answer will proceed, and any other relevant details on accommodations or registration. Moderators then should schedule a conference call with panelists.

"Some of the best panels I've ever seen are where the moderator had a pre-event conference call with all the panelists," says Sarah Sennett, a marketing executive at the Institution of Engineering and Technology. "The moderator found the particular strengths and specialties of each panelist within the subject matter, and pre-agreed on a few [subjects to cover] to ensure a balanced debate arose that sparked lots of questions from the floor." The key is to listen to the suggestions of the panel on your vision for the session. Having an open dialogue about it will help ensure an agenda that is well suited to participants, participants who are comfortable with the focus of the session, and, ultimately, a lively panel discussion.

A few days before the panel, reconfirm in writing, going into more logistical detail. Discuss what technology, if any, panelists will need. If they are using slides, get them in advance to ensure compatibility and ease of transition. Most importantly, provide directions to the venue and the time and location you'd like panelists to meet before the program, as well as a phone number where you can be reached at the last minute.

CRAFT AN AGENDA

A panel should have a detailed agenda. Craft it after the conference call, taking the specialties and suggestions of panelists into consideration. The exact time that each element of the panel will take place should be listed.

A PANEL SHOULD HAVE A DETAILED AGENDA.

Panelists should receive a copy of the agenda ahead of time so they know what to expect and how to prepare, such as opening remarks or responses to specific questions that the moderator will ask. Bring a copy for each panelist on the day of the session too and put it at his or her assigned seat.

Prepare and bring copies of back-up agendas. Consider crafting alternative agendas—one that is 15 or 30 minutes shorter than the time originally allotted. Because conferences often run late, this will allow you to help organizers get back on schedule. The other alternative agenda should account for a session that is one panelist short, so you can adjust for a last-minute cancellation.

WRITE SPEAKING MATERIAL

While an agenda is good outline, the moderator must also prepare what he or she will say at certain points in the panel. This speaking material doesn't have to be scripted; planned and rehearsed talking points work well. Don't forget to prepare:

AN OPENING

Get the attention of audience members with a catchy fact, statistic, quotation, anecdote, joke, or other relevant material. (See chapter 20 for more on attention-getting devices.) Then welcome the audience, thank panelists, link the opening line to the purpose of the panel, and preview how the panel will unfold (being explicit about when and how audience members can ask questions). The opening sets the tone for the entire panel; carefully craft and rehearse it until your delivery is smooth and enthusiastic.

INTRODUCTIONS

Moderators can craft the agenda so there is time to introduce all panelists during the beginning of the panel, or introduce each panelist right before he or she gives individual opening remarks.

Ask panelists to provide an introduction ahead of time. Most will send a page-long biography that must be shortened and made relevant to the panel discussion. A good introduction is about a minute long, highlights the most interesting and important aspects of a panelist's credentials, and provides a teaser of his or her remarks. An introduction also must include the preferred title and correct pronunciation of each panelist's name and affiliation. Practice it out loud. It doesn't count to say it in your head! (See chapter 29 for more on introducing a speaker.)

QUESTION & ANSWER/DISCUSSION

Plan in advance how and when you will solicit questions. Seed several questions with trusted audience members ahead of time. Ask one of them to volunteer a straightforward question immediately after you open the floor. This will prevent awkward silences, encourage others to ask questions, and get panelists comfortable responding. Other seeded questions can be interjected during lulls in the discussion. A good moderator has a list of questions prepared so he or she can open new topics of discussion during lulls as well.

Consider using low-tech pen and paper to invite questions from listeners. Or take advantage of high-tech tools such as Twitter or Facebook to solicit them. Plan how you will collect or access these questions and how you will intersperse them with live questions from the audience.

A CONCLUSION

Give notice that the panel is coming to a close by calling for the last audience question. After it is answered, pose a broad last question that allows each panelist to offer final thoughts or discuss future trends.

Then, thank the panelists, audience, event organizers, and, if appropriate, sponsors for providing a forum and engaging in a discussion on such an important issue. Share additional resources available to attendees and announce future events that may be of interest.

Link the conclusion to the catchy fact, statistic, quotation, anecdote, or joke you led with in the opening. If you have an evaluation form for the session, ask the audience to fill it out and express thanks for the feedback. Finally, if the panel is part of a larger conference, tell attendees what comes next and where they should go.

PREPARE TO FACILITATE THE DISCUSSION

Judy Hojel, the CEO at People and Performance Training, sums up the moderator's role, "A moderator is there to encourage interactivity between the audience and the panelists and the panelists themselves. The more relaxed they are, the more they encourage others to relax and therefore generate the best outcomes from each person.

"Being a good moderator means knowing when to bring in the participation of the audience, as well as knowing when to encourage the panelists to speak to each other," she adds.

Though effective moderators do much of their facilitating on the spot, they can practice relevant skills ahead of time, including:

LISTENING

Moderators need to listen carefully to interject follow-up questions, ask related questions of panelists who haven't been as involved in the conversation, and smoothly transition from speaker to speaker and topic to topic.

REPEATING AND REFRAMING

Moderators must repeat questions so that everyone can hear and panelists have a moment to formulate a response. The moderator should reframe a question if it is on a tangential topic or off base and steer it to a particular panelist who has particular expertise on the issue or who hasn't been as involved in the discussion.

After advance preparation is complete, don't forget these steps to follow on the day of your panel or group presentation to ensure it runs smoothly.

- Arrive early to set up. Put out an agenda, name placard, and glass of water for each panelist. Test microphones and other technology. Cue slides.

- Brief panelists 30 minutes before the panel. If they are a few minutes late for the briefing, they'll still be on time for the main event. Remind panelists how the session will unfold.

- Keep track of time. If panelists have opening remarks, set clear time limits beforehand. Find a trusted colleague or audience member to serve as the timer. Tell panelists during your briefing who will keep time, how time signals will be displayed, and how you will cut off panelists who go over time. Make sure the timekeeper is sitting where all panelists can see and provide cue cards that are large (i.e., hard to ignore).

- Start on time. Two minutes before the start of the panel, make an announcement that the session will begin shortly. Two minutes later, start the program. If attendees aren't seated, repeat a pleasantry, such as "good afternoon," several times and with long pauses between each repetition. A loud and enthusiastic greeting will be met with a quick response.

- End on time. No one likes a presentation that goes over time. Allow plenty of time for the final question and your wrap up. Concluding a few minutes early provides time for the audience to complete an evaluation and approach panelists.

- Follow up. After the event, send thank-you notes to the panelists, event organizer, timekeeper, and others who helped. Just like a party organizer, a gracious panel moderator won't have trouble getting volunteers to help put on an event in the future.

INTERRUPTING

Effective moderators must be skilled at interrupting politely. Doing so is key to keeping the agenda on track when a panelist has gone on too long during opening remarks or when answering a question. Audience members should be interrupted if they are using floor time to give a speech, not ask a question.

Interrupt kindly by waiting until the speaker is taking a breath or ending a sentence. Thank the speaker for his or her comments and indicate what it is time to move on to, such as the next panelist's opening remarks, another panelist's perspective, or a new question from the audience.

Moderating a panel truly is like hosting a celebration where someone else is the guest of honor. You won't need streamers or cake, but you will need careful preparation and a smooth delivery for everyone to feel comfortable and have a good time.

EXERCISE

Craft and deliver an hour-long group presentation with classmates or colleagues to explore a timely and relevant issue or to provide an overview of an industry issue (such as a quarterly or annual report). How did you tailor the topic to expected attendees? How did you prepare for your role? What was the most difficult aspect of moderating the panel or participating in it? What will you do differently to prepare for or present in a similar speaking role in the future?

ACTIVITY

Attend or watch a panel presentation (universities, think tanks, and industry conferences in your area are great places to find an upcoming panel presentation). What was the topic of the panel? Was it well selected for the audience? Were the panelists well selected? How effectively did the moderator facilitate the panel? What were his or her strengths? What could he or she have done differently? ▪

—— CHAPTER 29 ——

WHERE YOU SAY IT
Introducing a Speaker

It doesn't come during the speech, but it is vital to its success: the introduction of a speech. If you aren't putting together a formal introduction for someone to give before your speech or to give before remarks of a speaker featured at your event, at best, you're missing an opportunity, and at worst, you could be undermining the presentation.

Effective introductions tee up presentations. They highlight credentials, and thereby establish credibility before a word is uttered. They also provide a teaser of the content and smoothly transition to the featured speaker.

BIOGRAPHIES AND INTRODUCTIONS ARE NOT THE SAME AND SHOULD NOT BE USED INTERCHANGEABLY.

All too often, speakers and event organizers read a page-long biography for a speech introduction. Biographies and introductions are not the same and should not be used interchangeably. A biography is too long and detailed; it will bore audience members. It might even insult listeners by going on about the speaker's accomplishments and not mentioning what listeners will get from the upcoming presentation.

Here is what you need to know to craft an effective introduction for your next presentation or the next time you're introducing a speaker:

KEEP IT SHORT

An introduction is the prelude to the main event, not a stand-alone presentation. Thus, it is much shorter than a biography or speech; aim for three or four sentences that take from one to two minutes to read.

TALK ABOUT THE PAST, PRESENT, AND FUTURE

In terms of the past, pick the most relevant credentials to mention. Highlight accomplishments that will resonate with audience members and be sure to keep it brief. Include the present in your introduction, meaning the speaker's current work and affiliations. Just as importantly, look to the immediate future by giving audience members a teaser of the content and a glimpse of how they stand to benefit by listening to the presentation. Going from past and present to future helps build excitement and capture attention. Make sure you confirm the speaker's preferred title (Dr., Ms., Mrs., etc.), as well as the correct pronunciation of his or her name and other proper nouns (such as a hometown or educational institution) that you plan to mention in the introduction.

TAILOR MATERIAL

Every introduction should be specific to the audience, occasion, and moment in time. Speaking at an academic conference? Mention degrees, affiliations, and a relevant journal publication to bolster credibility. Speaking at a conference of entrepreneurs? Skip the academic detail and focus on key business successes or awards and memberships in professional associations that are respected among entrepreneurs. The specific speech topic and reason for the audience to care should always be unique.

MAKE IT EASY TO READ

Because an introduction is short in duration and rich in detail, it is one of the few speaking situations where scripted remarks do make sense. Read the introduction aloud several times to ensure it flows smoothly and sounds

SAMPLE SPEECHES OF INTRODUCTION

Introductions can and should be given for presentations in many contexts—formal speeches, routine business meetings, and even social events. Here are some examples:

An introduction for presentation skills workshop

"Our next presenter has spent the last five years transforming experts into leaders with presentation-skills, workshops, and coaching sessions offered through her company, Spoken with Authority. She also teaches public speaking at the George Washington University and is a regular contributor to *Toastmasters Magazine*, the official publication of Toastmasters International.

"Today, to help us prepare for our speaking roles at the upcoming annual meeting, she will reveal the five secrets of speaking with confidence and the principles of crafting effective professional presentations. Please help me welcome Christine Clapp."

An introduction at a business meeting

"Alex Smith, who has been the communications director at Acme for 15 years and is in the process of implementing our marketing plan, will present three options for new website vendors this afternoon. Let me turn it over to Alex."

An introduction at a celebration

"At this time, Charlie Washington, the groom's roommate when he was an undergraduate at Willamette University, will lead us in a toast to the newlyweds."

conversational. Print it in large font (at least 20 point), double space it, and only print it on the top two-thirds of each page (so you don't have to drop your chin down as far when you read). It's a good idea to prepare an introduction for your own speech. Sent a draft ahead of time to the person introducing you. Bring an extra copy on the day of your speech.

TRANSITION TO THE SPEAKER

All introductions should build in excitement, culminating with a smooth transition to the featured speaker. In formal situations, request the audience to join in welcoming the speaker to the lectern. When you are delivering introductory remarks, take a step back from the lectern after you read your script, turn to the speaker with a smile on your face, and reach out to shake the speaker's hand when he or she reaches the lectern. Such a transition will avoid an awkward moment and will help increase the speaker's level of comfort and confidence at the beginning of his or her presentation.

With a small investment in time, you can craft an introduction that adds tremendous value to a presentation by positioning the speaker as an expert, providing a reason for listeners to pay attention, and bolstering the speaker's confidence—all before a word of the featured speech is delivered.

EXERCISE

Prepare a one-minute introduction for a presentation you are giving in a professional or educational context. Have a classmate or colleague read the introduction before you speak. What impact did the introduction have on the overall presentation? How did it influence your level of preparedness or confidence?

ACTIVITY

Award shows are probably the most publicized arena where introductions occur. Some introductions are short and sweet, others long and drawn out. Search for award show introductions (the Mark Twain Prize for Humor is a good one) and watch how the presenters attempt to strike a balance between being humorous and being sincere about the person being introduced. Are there common elements related to timing or structure that make for a good introduction? How can you translate those to your own speaking? ▪

— CHAPTER 30 —

WHERE YOU SAY IT
Question & Answer and Impromptu Speaking

All too often, question and answer sessions (Q&A) are neglected in texts on professional presentation skills. But they are an important and common type of speaking, also known as impromptu speaking, that you will need to master for career success. (See chapter 9 for more on the four modes of speaking, including the impromptu mode.)

After all, job interviews are a type of Q&A session; so are media interviews and town-hall meetings. Question and answer sessions also can come at the end of a speaking event, such as a keynote speech, meeting, client pitch, conference panel, or training seminar.

Here are some guidelines for answering questions with confidence and ease:

THINK OF IT AS PUBLIC SPEAKING

Think of Q&A as public speaking because that's what it is. Sometimes speakers let down their guard during question and answer sessions—their posture relaxes and vocal projection suffers, they use more "ums" and other junk words, and use repetitive gestures to talk with their hands. True, question and answer sessions can be less formal than delivering prepared remarks. But you still should convey confidence with your posture, expressions, and gestures, and work to avoid distracting sounds and movements that detract from your message.

PREPARE

Even though you likely won't know the exact questions in advance of an impromptu speaking situation, you can still make educated guesses about what will be asked. Research and prepare responses to expected questions, as well as a few worst-case-scenario questions that you are most nervous about getting. Then, practice your answers at least six times, or until you can easily recall and articulate the responses.

In cases where Q&A is the main attraction, such as job and media interviews, identify two or three main themes or messages you want listeners to take away from your responses. Brainstorm and rehearse anecdotes that highlight the themes and link your answers to them when possible. (See more on this job interview technique in chapter 31.)

RESEARCH AND PREPARE RESPONSES TO EXPECTED QUESTIONS, AS WELL AS A FEW WORST-CASE-SCENARIO QUESTIONS THAT YOU ARE MOST NERVOUS ABOUT GETTING.

The goal is to control the interview by bridging questions to responses that are memorable and consistent with your overall message. Note, however, that not every question can be answered with a prepared, on-point response. The more practice and experience you get with Q&A, the more often and artfully you will be able to link questions to material you want to share and to control the interview.

PAUSE

Give yourself a moment to think before responding to questions. Many speakers rush into an answer without taking a moment to think it through. A five- or 10-second pause is perfectly acceptable and will help prevent a rambling response. Listeners would rather have a thoughtful response than an immediate and rambling one. Take a drink of water when you need a longer pause. Get comfortable formulating your thoughts in silence; don't use junk words to fill the pause.

THE ART OF *ASKING* A QUESTION

The person answering questions isn't the only one with a speaking role during a question and answer session—the people asking questions are presenting too. Don't forget some basic rules for asking questions:

Ask a question

It seems obvious, but all-too-often doesn't happen. A pointed question is fine, but this is not the time to deliver a monologue.

Be brief

Shorten the personal story that leads into your question. Q&A isn't the time to seek assistance with your individual issue, but rather it's a time to use your personal experience as the basis to ask a question that is relevant to fellow audience members.

Avoid reading

Asking a question can cause as much nervousness as delivering a speech. But rather than scripting and reading your question, prepare and rehearse it ahead of time. It is great practice for presenting in a concise and conversational manner while nervous.

Project your voice

In many situations, a microphone isn't available for people asking questions during question and answer sessions. Remember to speak especially loudly, slowly, and clearly so the speaker, as well as other audience members, can hear your question.

Stay standing

Stand up when you ask your question and remain standing while it is answered. It will help you project your voice and will allow the speaker to make eye contact with you while answering your question.

SHOW GRATITUDE

Thank the interviewer or audience member for questions. You don't have to do it for each and every question in a long Q&A session, but do it enough to build rapport with listeners.

It is especially helpful to thank a hostile questioner in a genuine manner because it can diffuse tension. Don't repeat the negative charge or accusation, but pick out the issue being addressed. For example, "Thank you for bringing up the issue of cost because I know it's a real concern in this economy." Another subtle way to show gratitude and respect is to respond to the questioner by name during your answer.

RESTATE THE QUESTION

Speakers should repeat questions to show they understand. If you are unclear about what was asked, don't hesitate to request clarification from the questioner. Also, when you have a large audience, repeating audience questions allows everyone to hear what was asked.

But even in a one-on-one interview, restating the question can be helpful because you can reframe it when necessary—to diffuse a hostile question or to bridge the question to a related subject you want to discuss.

Just be careful when linking a question to another topic—it has to be in the ballpark or listeners will feel insulted. And honesty is the best policy; if you don't know, don't try to fake it. Offer to follow up with the questioner with specific information that you don't know off the top of your head or that falls outside your area of expertise.

BE CONCISE

Don't filibuster during question and answer sessions. Listener attention can wane and it means fewer questions can be addressed. Most responses in Q&A sessions should run about one to two minutes long, but the length of your answer should depend first and foremost on how long it takes to fully answer the question. If you can respond in a sentence or two, no need to stretch it out. If you need longer to tell a story, provide a few examples or offer an analogy (that is fine too).

Don't pay short shrift to impromptu speaking and specifically Q&A sessions. They are a common and important format for speakers to master.

EXERCISE

The best impromptu answer to a question is planned well in advance. Although paradoxical, belief in this statement will better prepare you for answering questions. Review an outline of a presentation you expect to deliver and consider the presentation from the perspective of audience members. Write down five questions you would expect to get from listeners. Then, enlist the help of three expected audience members. Have them review your outline or draft remarks and write down five questions they might ask in a Q&A session for that presentation. What was the most common question? How might you edit your presentation to address it during your remarks? Did your list of questions overlap with expected audience members? What questions from expected listeners were most surprising and how could you respond to them?

ACTIVITY

Watch a recording of an American presidential debate (either between nominees at the party level or nominees who are squaring off before a national election) or watch an Intelligence Squared debate on a contemporary issue (www.intelligencesquared.com). Which speakers were most effective and natural in their off-the-cuff responses to questions? What specific behaviors did they exhibit? Describe an example of a failed response to a question. Why didn't it resonate? How could the speaker have done it differently? What did you learn in the analysis of the debate that you could apply to your next impromptu speaking situation or Q&A session? ▪

——— CHAPTER 31 ———

WHERE YOU SAY IT
Job Interviews

American novelist Daniel Handler, better known by the pen name Lemony Snicket, once wrote, "Besides getting several paper cuts in the same day or receiving the news that someone in your family has betrayed you to your enemies, one of the most unpleasant experiences in life is a job interview." Alas, it is a task that workers today must do on a somewhat regular basis; the Bureau of Labor Statistics estimates the average worker today stays at each job just 4.4 years.[1]

The next time you are in the process of interviewing for a position or promotion, rethink your interview strategy: Approach it as an opportunity to sell who you are, not what you know.

APPROACH A JOB INTERVIEW AS AN OPPORTUNITY TO SELL WHO YOU ARE, NOT WHAT YOU KNOW.

Conventional wisdom says the purpose of an interview is to elaborate on qualifications—what you know. But employers don't waste time interviewing candidates who don't meet basic requirements. They use your resume to make this judgment.

In the vast majority of cases, you are already deemed qualified when you are asked for a phone or in-person interview. The interview, then, is really about finding out if you are a good fit in terms of personality.

Here are three steps that will help you sell who you are during your next job interview:

IDENTIFY KEY STRENGTHS

Come up with three adjectives that you want the interviewer to associate with you. These qualities should position you, not only as a good fit for the job, but also as the best candidate out there.

Make sure the adjectives set you apart and speak to your personality. Interviewers hear from many candidates who say they're hard workers or team players, but they likely don't hear from many candidates who say they are competitive, resilient, or observant.

If you have a competitive spirit and having the drive to win is an asset in the position you're interviewing for, then it should be one of the themes you go back to in the stories you share during your interview. Same goes for resiliency or perceptiveness.

The point is that you should avoid common, trite, or "stock" responses that many candidates will give about their personal traits or strengths. Stand out from the crowd; strategically identify

HEARTY HANDSHAKES

In addition to standing tall, smiling, and wearing professional clothing, your handshake is an important aspect of the first impression you make at job interviews, networking events, and meetings. Here are a few guidelines to ensure your handshake conveys both confidence and respect:

Go in strong

Without hesitation, extend your right hand just above your waist level to initiate a handshake with the person you are meeting. Your fingers should be together, but not tense. And you palm and fingers should be perpendicular to the ground and your thumb should be almost parallel to the ground.

Lean in to the handshake. If you are a few steps away, take a small step in the direction of the person with whom you are shaking hands to avoid an extended or awkward handshake.

Grip firmly

You don't want to be a bone crusher or to inflict pain on the person with whom you are shaking hands, but you do want your handshake to be very firm. A limp handshake can be read as a sign of a lack of confidence.

Unless you are a rock climber or athlete with exceptional grip strength, it's best to grasp the other person's hand harder than you think you should. And make sure you aren't gripping just the other person's fingers; your fingers should cover the top to the other person's hand and your thumb should touch his or her palm.

Double pump and release

Once you are firmly gripping the hand of the person you are meeting, pump your hand up and down two times in a firm, controlled fashion. Then release the handshake and return your right hand to your side. Avoid going up too high (the motion of the handshake should only be a few inches up and down). Avoid shaking too many times (two up and downs is standard). Avoid going to fast (a rushed, jerky handshake is a sign of nervousness).

HEARTY HANDSHAKES
(continued)

Also, be respectful of personal space. Generally avoid touching the other person on the shoulder or arm with your left hand or going in for a hug unless the other person initiates the contact.

You can mirror an additional point of contact if you are comfortable doing so, but should avoid initiating it to prevent an awkward or uncomfortable situation.

Look and smile

As you are initiating and executing the handshake, hold eye contact with the person you're greeting and smile at him or her. Don't rush things. Take time to really look, smile, and connect when you are engaging in a handshake.

Offer a greeting

When you are meeting someone for the first time or if the person may not remember you, say your first and last name slowly, loudly, and clearly. If you have met before or are connected in another way, it is helpful to provide context, "I'm Quinn Smith from Generic Consulting Group. We met last year at the Leadership Summit in Chicago."

Always err on the side of caution in offering your name and context; better to say it as a reminder to the person you are greeting than assume he or she remembers.

The time that you are shaking hands with someone is also a good time to ask the proper pronunciation of the other person's name or to have them remind you what it is if they do not offer it, and to provide the proper pronunciation of your name if it was repeated incorrectly.

Following these handshake guidelines will help ensure you make a great impression the next time you are meeting someone new or greeting an old acquaintance.

some unique traits about yourself that could be an asset in the position for which you are interviewing. It's better to be rejected for being authentic and different, rather than boring and safe. Besides, you have a much better chance of success when you are authentic and different.

IDENTIFY KEY EXPERIENCES

Next, think of at least three important experiences in your life that have shaped who you are. Such experiences might include your hometown or state, sports you played growing up, family, schools you attended, volunteer work you enjoyed, jobs you've held in the past, hobbies, or travel you've done. You may identify many more than three experiences, and that is great.

Remember not to limit yourself to paid employment here. This is one of the biggest mistakes job seekers make. Formative experiences often happen outside the office and should be discussed in a job interview.

There's a good chance that most, if not all, of the important life experiences you identify are missing from your resume, or would take an extremely careful reading to tease out. Don't leave it up to the interviewer to read between the lines of your resume to figure out who you are and what you value.

BRAINSTORM STORIES

Once you have identified your key strengths and experiences, then it is time to brainstorm specific stories highlighting them to use to respond to interview questions. Come up with and rehearse about a dozen, which means you will have a few possible stories to tell for each trait and experience. Some anecdotes might even touch on several traits and experiences.

During your interview, you likely won't use the all the stories you identified beforehand. But having an inventory of anecdotes that you have rehearsed will give you lots of fodder to answer the different types of questions that could come up in your interview.

If asked directly in an interview what your greatest strengths are and what experiences have shaped you, you certainly could rattle off the list of three traits and three or more experiences. But your interviewer no doubt will have a better chance of remembering several well-told anecdotes that highlight those themes than recalling a list of adjectives and experiences that have no context.

And stories are more believable. It's one thing to claim you possess a trait, but to provide evidence in the form of a specific story is another. This advice isn't different from what you may have heard in the past about the importance of quantifying successes during an interview. It'll just be more powerful because the "data" is shared as part of a story. (See chapter 17 for more on storytelling.)

It requires practice and discipline to bridge, or artfully segue, the question an interviewer asks to a story you want to tell. The goal is to control the message in your responses such that at the end of the interview, the person or people interviewing you have written down on their notepads your key traits and life experiences, and remember a few of the stories you told to highlight those traits and experiences. (See more on impromptu speaking in chapter 30.)

Remember: Sell what you know on your resume; sell who you are in the job interview. Being clear about who you are in an interview helps ensure a good employment fit. You have a greater chance of thriving professionally when your personality meshes with the position and organization. And you might just find yourself avoiding the experience of interviewing for a job every 4.4 years.

EXERCISE

Create a list of five questions that you have received in a past job interview or that you think might come up in the future. Prepare and rehearse one to two minute answers to each of the questions. Work on being concise and sharing personal anecdotes that speak to your key strengths and experiences in your answers.

ACTIVITY

There are many different approaches to job interviews from the interviewer's perspective. Some interviewers create a combative environment to see how you respond to stress. Others might try to be very nice to you in order to see who you are when your guard is down. Before your next job interview, ask a friend, classmate, or colleague to interview you wearing the hats of the friendly interviewer and the hard-ball interviewer. Knowing you can handle different situations will help reduce your anxiety and prevent you from being caught off guard. It might even be the reason you get your next job. ▪

1. "Employee Tenure in 2012," *Bureau of Labor Statistics.* U.S. Department of Labor. 18 September 2012. Web. 2 December 2013.

—————— CHAPTER 32 ——————

WHERE YOU SAY IT
Networking and Social Events

Perhaps you've heard that you should have a minute long "elevator speech" ready in case you serendipitously hop on an elevator with the CEO of the company where you've always wanted to work or the key investor you've been pursuing to help you get a new venture off the ground. Maybe you've even given some thought to how you'd introduce yourself if you ever have that once-in-a-lifetime chance meeting in the elevator. But if you're like many professionals, you assume you'll never encounter that sort of situation, so you haven't worried about preparing an elevator speech.

You're probably right about never needing to pitch yourself in an elevator. But you certainly will need to introduce yourself at networking events, conferences, social functions, and even job interviews—anywhere you're asked "Tell me about yourself" or "What do you do?" If you're not approaching these everyday situations as opportunities to give a strategic introduction of yourself, you're missing opportunities to grow both professionally and personally. Your elevator speech is an essential tool for marketing yourself.

Just because you're introducing yourself in a conversational or small-group setting doesn't mean you should wing it. In fact, you should prepare and rehearse your elevator speech to an audience of one with as much care as you would prepare and rehearse a conference keynote to an audience of a thousand.

When you approach the crafting of your elevator speech as you would a formal speech, it means that you need to prepare strategically, rehearse thoroughly, receive feedback, and rework material if it's not achieving the results you want. But it doesn't mean your elevator speech should be scripted, stiff, or unchanging. On the contrary, it should include three key elements that are covered conversationally and can be adapted to fit the specific situation you're in.

The three key elements of a memorable elevator speech are:

DESCRIBE YOURSELF AS A SOLUTION TO A PROBLEM

The most important part of your elevator speech is the first sentence. When you don't have much time, this sentence becomes the short version of your elevator speech. And even when you do have a minute or two for the long version of your elevator speech, the first sentence will determine whether the person or people you're talking to will continue listening or if they'll tune you out.

For that important first sentence then, make sure you describe yourself as a solution to a problem faced by your clients, customers, or colleagues. Listeners don't necessarily care what your job title is or how your industry describes the work you do. They want to know how you can help them solve a problem.

"I now introduce myself as a person who provides solutions for individuals experiencing a variety of speech and language disorders," said Raleen A. Miller, a speech-language pathologist at Metropolitan Speech Pathology Group in Washington, D.C., and a member of the George Washington University Toastmasters Club, who learned to talk about what problems she solves, rather than what she does, when meeting prospective clients. "Yes, I do provide direct therapy as a speech-language pathologist, but that's not the first thing I talk about, it's the last."

Remember, when crafting the first line of your elevator speech, you need to answer for people you're introducing yourself to the age-old question, "What's in it for me?" Getting to the bottom line in plain terms will ensure listeners engage with you and that their eyes don't glaze over as you recite your official title, certifications, or other jargon.

TELL AN ANECDOTE

After you describe how you solve a problem for the people you work with, tell a short story to explain your motivation for doing what you do. This anecdote should be a "signature story"—one that reveals the ah-ha moment when you realized you wanted to do what you do or an example that shows that how exceptional you are at your craft.

Santi Bhagat, the founder and president of Physician-Parent Caregivers (PPC), a non-profit organization that advocates for quality healthcare for children and young adults with chronic conditions and disabilities, admitted that "as a physician, my natural inclination is to speak in clinical mode, even when I'm talking about the experience of my daughter's chronic illness that spurred the creation of PPC.

"I now understand the power of storytelling and weave my daughter's story into my personal introduction and PPC's calls for changes in the health policy and medical worlds. Too often, we think numbers and data make the case for our listeners, but it's really the image of a real person that makes them care."

The value of telling an anecdote is that people enjoy listening to stories (just think of kids at bedtime), they are more memorable than highlights from a resume (people at networking events don't always remember a name, but they can recount an interesting narrative), and they build rapport with listeners (opening up by sharing a personal story will help establish a connection even with someone you just met). (See more in chapter 17 on storytelling.)

Remember that your anecdote must be brief—your entire elevator speech should be just one to two minutes long. It should have a few specific details to make the story interesting and colorful. And it should include vivid language that adds texture and drama to your story.

START A DIALOGUE

Finally, end with an open-ended question—one that can't be answered with a simple "yes" or "no." The ultimate goal of an elevator speech is to not to give a monologue, but to start a dialogue. After all, you can't learn about someone you just met while your lips are moving. You have to let your ears do the work.

Carolyn Semedo had the right idea when it comes to the ultimate goal of an elevator speech, "Closing with a question draws the listener in, creating a dialogue that can serve as the foundation for a deeper conversation and, eventually, a relationship."

This is a realistic expectation for an elevator speech. Though you likely won't land a job or close a sale after giving your one to two minute introduction, it is feasible to make a connection that leads to further conversation and collaboration.

The question you ask at the end of your introduction can be as simple as, "And what is it that you do?" Or, depending on the occasion, you can make it more specific to your field of work or the type of person you are networking with. Above all else, your question must show you are interested in learning more about the person you're meeting.

The content of a memorable elevator speech should be brief: position yourself as a solution to a problem, share a personal anecdote that explains why you do what you do, and transform your introduction from a monologue to a dialogue. Make sure you prepare, rehearse, and regularly revisit your elevator speech to effectively market yourself and capitalize on opportunities that come your way—whether you're in an elevator, or not!

HERE ARE A FEW QUESTIONS YOU CAN USE AT NETWORKING EVENTS TO START A CONVERSATION OR KEEP THE DIALOGUE GOING:

- This is a beautiful venue, have you been to an event here before?

- I don't get to this part of town much, but it really is nice. Do you work nearby?

- How did you hear about this event? Are you a member of the host organization?

- How did you end up in this line of work?

- What do you like most about your industry/company/job?

SAMPLE ELEVATOR SPEECH

"I'm Christine Clapp and through my business, *Spoken with Authority,* I transform subject experts into thought leaders.

"When I was a college freshman, I had to participate in debate as a requirement of my major. After a humiliating defeat to a top team from Pacific Lutheran University, I dedicated myself to becoming an excellent speaker and empowering others with communication skills.

"What challenges have you faced as a speaker?"

EXERCISE

Brainstorm three different ways you could craft the first line of your elevator speech, for when you describe yourself in terms of a solution to a problem faced by the people you work for or with. Share your drafted opening lines to your elevator speech with three trusted colleagues, classmates, or friends. Which opening line resonated with them most? Why? How could you make that line more catchy and compelling, such that it would be memorable and help spur conversation?

ACTIVITY

Attend a networking event, paying attention to the introductions given by the new people you meet. Whose introduction was most interesting or memorable? Whose was boring or unintelligible? How did a person's introduction impact your conversation with him or her? What can you learn from your analysis of the introductions you encountered at the networking event that you can apply to your own personal introduction/elevator speech? ▪

—————— CHAPTER 33 ——————

WHERE YOU SAY IT
Evaluations and Performance Appraisals

Evaluations are a double-edged sword: If you are too harsh, you will dishearten or alienate the person you are evaluating; but if you are too glowing, you will rob the person you are evaluating of an opportunity to learn and grow.

Giving evaluations is a part of professional life. Just think of the last time that your boss asked for feedback on a presentation or you had to provide a performance review to a subordinate. And the ability to evaluate effectively becomes more important as you climb the corporate ladder and take on leadership roles. Here are several suggestions to help you strike the right balance of honesty and tact in your evaluations:

START WITH A POSITIVE

Just like any other presentation, an evaluation should have an introduction, body, and conclusion. Start on a positive note in your introduction. You might acknowledge a specific strength of the person you are evaluating or point out an area in which he or she has shown improvement. Either way, you are building rapport and improving the likelihood that the subject of your evaluation will be receptive to your suggestions.

There are situations in which beginning positively is not appropriate. For example, if an employee has been reviewed several times and continues to make the same mistakes or if an error is egregious, then a positive comment might mask the gravity of the situation. In these cases, one should begin by summarizing the past evaluations or reviewing the circumstances of the error. This builds a strong foundation for the criticism provided in the next part of the evaluation.

HAVE STRUCTURE IN THE BODY OF YOUR EVALUATION AND PREVIEW IT

As you proceed into the body of your evaluation, provide the person you are evaluating a preview of how you are going to move through your feedback. Some evaluators just go through a list of items, which can feel chaotic or even overwhelming.

Aim to structure your evaluation under two or three general topics, which serve as main points. If you are evaluating a speech, you might give feedback on content and delivery. For a performance review, you might center your evaluation on the three key responsibilities of the employee, such as greeting customers, processing orders, and updating the website.

Then, break each topic into two components. First, share one thing the person you are evaluating did well. Then, suggest one thing that he or she needs to focus on as an area needing improvement. For top performers, you might need to discuss one thing they did well but could have done even better, or one thing they have improved upon but still could work on. This will help ensure that you don't provide a "whitewash"—an evaluation that is filled with positives but has no helpful suggestions for improvement.

And in the case of someone who is struggling, select your feedback strategically. You want to tackle areas needing the most improvement first. Then, as the person addresses those issues, you can turn to less crucial needs in future feedback sessions.

BE SPECIFIC AND TROUBLESHOOT

For an evaluation to be effective, it must be specific. For example, if you are praising an employee's manner in greeting customers, tell him or her exactly what you like, "You do a great job making customers feel welcome when they walk in the door by smiling, making direct eye contact, introducing yourself, and offering your assistance in finding anything." If you aren't specific, the person might not know the exact elements of his or her greeting that you find admirable.

IF YOU STOP AT IDENTIFYING A PROBLEM, YOU CAN DEFLATE AND OVERWHELM THE PERSON YOU ARE EVALUATING.

And, when you identify areas to improve, make sure to troubleshoot. Take for example the customer greeter, "At times, your greetings can be difficult for customers to hear. To improve your intelligibility, I would like to see you project your voice more effectively by standing taller and speaking from your diaphragm. I have an article with more detail on proper vocal projection that I will e-mail you after our meeting. Also, you can hold off on your greeting until you have walked closer to the customer, which will make it easier for him or her to hear."

If you stop at identifying a problem, you can deflate and overwhelm the person you are evaluating. Serve as a mentor; provide actionable suggestions on how to address the problem and improve performance.

CONCLUDE BY SUMMARIZING AND EVOKING YOUR INTRODUCTION

When you move to your conclusion, review the main points of your evaluation. Then, recall the positive detail you used during your introduction and end with a challenge to reach greater heights. It can be as simple as, "I want to thank you again for streamlining our order processing procedures and I look forward to hearing more of your ideas on how we can better serve our customers."

This structure ensures that you are sandwiching the entire evaluation with an upbeat opening and conclusion.

Following these tips can help you hit the sweet spot between being too harsh and too glowing in your feedback. Finding this balance in evaluations will make you that much more valuable as an employee and effective as a manager.

EXERCISE

When asked to give feedback to a teacher, professor, supervisor, etc., use the opportunity to practice effective evaluation skills. If there is a comment section on an evaluation form, offer your feedback of the person or program in the form prescribed above. The subject of your evaluation will appreciate it.

ACTIVITY

We all get evaluated. None of us want to be belittled or berated. With this in mind, craft and deliver an oral evaluation of your last presentation. As you are evaluating yourself, put yourself in an impartial frame of mind. Be legitimately critical of yourself, but don't lose track of how you would want to be evaluated: the tone, the language choices, the level of detail, and the concrete suggestions for improvement. ▪

—————— CHAPTER 34 ——————

WHERE YOU SAY IT
Award Ceremonies

In March 1985, actress Sally Field won her second Oscar for Best Actress based on her role in the film *Places in the Heart*. Her often-mocked acceptance speech ended with the following lines:

> This means so much more to me this time, I don't know why. I think the first time I hardly felt it because it was all so new. But I want to say thank you to you. I haven't had an orthodox career. And I've wanted more than anything to have your respect. The first time I didn't feel it. But this time I feel it. And I can't deny the fact that you like me, right now, you like me!

This chapter is aimed at helping participants at award ceremonies—those who receive awards and those who present them—deliver remarks that will be remembered for all the right reasons.

FOR AWARD RECIPIENTS

PREPARE REMARKS

On some occasions, award recipients don't know they are even being considered for an award. They are forced to give an impromptu acceptance speech. More often than not, however, recipients know ahead of time that they were nominated or selected for an honor. Impromptu speaking should not be used in these situations.

When you have been selected or nominated in advance, there is no excuse for an unprepared acceptance speech. Listeners will expect a good measure of polish in your remarks. And you should seize the opportunity to plan and rehearse an acceptance speech that you won't later regret (either for being embarrassing or for overlooking an important thank you).

Some think it is bad luck to prepare remarks to accept an award for which one is nominated. But it is better to have remarks that go unused than to wing your moment in the spotlight. And don't just scribble a few words on a napkin before the award is announced. Practice your planned acceptance speech at least six times aloud before the event so you can deliver it largely without notes. It will not be memorized, but your key points will be. If anything, you may want a small slip of paper or one notecard in your pocket with a few words or names written down to refer to if you are nervous, excited, or emotional and need the crutch.

And if you do get emotional in the moment, don't worry. It is OK to cry. But don't sob your way through the speech, making it unintelligible. Stop speaking, glance down at your notes while you regain composure, and look back up at audience members when you are able to continue.

EXPRESS GRATITUDE

For the content of your acceptance speech, start by thanking the organization that honored you. Acknowledge the organization's accomplishments or importance.

Then, express gratitude for receiving the award. Remember to show humility—something Sally Field lacked at the Oscars in 1985. On the other hand, never say that you don't deserve the award; that could come across as ungrateful or even disrespectful to the organization that selected you for it or others who were considered for it.

Finally, recognize the key person or people who were formative or helpful in your development, as it relates to the award. You might mention a mentor or maybe your closest family members. But do not let your acceptance speech become a laundry list of names—your audience will get bored and your gratitude will come across as less sincere.

In the same vein, keep your remarks short. A two- to three-minute speech is appropriate on most occasions. You may be expected to speak longer for an award that you have been told about in advance, such as a lifetime-achievement award. Confirm your allotted speaking time with the event organizer in these situations.

DON'T ABUSE YOUR TIME IN THE SPOTLIGHT. IT CAN BE TEMPTING TO USE THIS OCCASION TO RAISE AWARENESS OF AN ISSUE OR FURTHER YOUR PERSONAL AGENDA. BUT DON'T TURN AN ACCEPTANCE SPEECH INTO A POLICY SPEECH.

Finally, don't abuse your time in the spotlight. It can be tempting to use this occasion to raise awareness of an issue or further your personal agenda. But don't turn an acceptance speech into a policy speech. Actor Marlon Brando made this mistake in March 1973 when he refused the Best Actor Oscar for his portrayal of Vito Corleone in *The Godfather.* He boycotted the award ceremony and sent Sacheen Littlefeather, a civil rights activist, to present a message that explained his reasons, which centered on the depiction of American Indians in the film industry. The move was criticized widely.

ACCEPT THE AWARD WITH GRACE

When your name has been called to accept an award, don't dilly-dally. You'll have plenty of time to shake hands and hug friends after the ceremony—avoid doing much of it on the way to the podium.

When you get to the podium, take care with the steps so you don't trip, and walk with purpose to the lectern. If the person giving the award is holding it for you, take the award in your left hand and shake the presenter's hand with your right. If photographers are capturing the moment, make sure to hold the handshake, turning your body toward the audience and holding the award up for all to see.

Then, get settled. Place the award on the lectern when possible so you don't distract listeners by fiddling with it or gesturing with it during your speech. Also, pause while the presenter is walking away from the lectern and audience members are concluding their applause. Remember to smile and look out at the crowd before you start your acceptance speech.

And at the conclusion of your acceptance speech, it is customary to stand at the lectern smiling until the emcee of the event comes toward you to shake hands or you are escorted off the stage. Standing silent in the spotlight likely will feel awkward, but try to embrace the moment. Smile and take in the audience applause graciously.

FOR AWARD PRESENTERS

SCRIPT REMARKS

This handbook generally advocates the use of the extemporaneous mode of speaking because it promotes a conversational delivery and eye contact, to name just a few reasons (see chapter 9 for more details). But speakers who are presenting an award generally are well served by writing out their remarks word-for-word. Scripting makes sense in cases like this, when the presentation is short and includes a good deal of specific information.

EXPLAIN THE AWARD AND SHARE ANECDOTES ABOUT THE RECIPIENT

When it comes to the content of the award presentation, make sure you provide an explanation of the award (what it is for and why it is important) as well as its history (how long it has been given and notable past recipients).

Then, pay tribute to the person being honored. You may include a few biographical details and mention key accomplishments. But keep this material brief so you can spend the bulk of your time sharing specific anecdotes and examples of the recipient's work that make him or her an appropriate honoree. The goal is to demonstrate why the recipient is worthy to audience members who may not be familiar with his or her work. A few well-selected stories can go a long way toward making the point in an interesting and memorable way.

DON'T FORGET TO IDENTIFY AND PRACTICE THE CORRECT PRONUNCIATION OF THE RECIPIENT'S NAME.

Some award presenters withhold the recipient's name until the end of their presentation to add suspense. Others reveal the recipient's name before speaking about him or her. Either way is fine. Just make sure to respect the tradition of the event and wishes of the event organizers before scripting your presentation. And on the subject of naming the award winner, don't forget to identify and practice the correct pronunciation of the recipient's name.

WELCOME THE RECIPIENT TO THE LECTERN

At the conclusion of the presentation of the award, you should welcome the recipient to the lectern. Begin by smiling warmly and leading audience members in applause. Continue smiling and clapping as the award recipient makes his or her way to the lectern. Remember to avoid clapping into the microphone because it can hurt the ears of audience members.

Then, as the recipient nears the lectern, take a few steps back from the lectern and a few steps in the direction of the award winner as you hold the award in both hands. When he or she is a few steps away, shift the award to your left hand and extend your right hand for a handshake. If photographers are capturing the moment on film, pause during the handshake and presentation of the award. Don't forget to smile at the camera, which will cue the award recipient to pose too. After pictures are taken, turn control of the award to the recipient and guide him or her to the lectern.

Finally, move briskly to the side of the stage or off the stage if you are not the event emcee. You want to melt into the background as applause is winding down so your award recipient can take center stage.

You never want to be mocked for your performance at an award ceremony, whether for your acceptance or presentation of an award. These tips above will ensure that you won't.

EXERCISE

Make up an award and identify someone you know who is deserving of it. Craft and deliver a two to three minute award presentation speech that explains the award, identifies the recipient of the award, and tells why he or she is worthy of the honor.

Then, take that speech and revise one element to make it stand out. Your goal is to make one aspect of the speech memorable. This might come through additional attention to style or by defying a convention of the genre. Once you have made this revision, deliver it to a trusted friend, colleague, or classmate, and ask for feedback about that element in particular.

ACTIVITY

Watch two award shows, such as the Academy Awards, Golden Globes, Screen Actors Guild, Tony Awards, Mark Twain Prize for American Humor, MTV Video Music Awards, Grammy Awards, etc., paying attention to acceptance speeches. Which acceptance speeches were most appropriate? Most memorable? Why? How do you think a noteworthy award recipient prepared his or her acceptance speech? Was the preparation adequate? Was his or her speech a good fit for the tone of the event? How could it have been more effective? ▪

———— CHAPTER 35 ————

WHERE YOU SAY IT
Toasts

Actress Anne Hathaway once said, "Weddings are important because they celebrate life and possibility." The toasts given on these joyous occasions should add to, and not detract from, the celebration. Unfortunately, there are those who wing it, who ramble, who tell inappropriate stories about the groom, who offer the entire life story of the bride, or who drink too much before taking the microphone and embarrass everyone. For as simple as it seems to give a great toast, it can be harder to give these brief, heartfelt speeches than to give a well-researched work presentation or conference keynote.

It's no wonder that many speakers struggle with them. Toasts are given at weddings and at other special occasions to people we care about deeply; we have something important to say and only a few minutes to say it. In many ways, the stakes are higher.

CRAFTING A TOAST

Here are the basics of crafting a toast that will be remembered for all the right reasons:

PLAN AHEAD

Don't wing it. Prepare an outline and rehearse it at least six times—or until you can deliver it comfortably without notes. You don't have to convey your thoughts word for word—just memorize the main ideas and rehearse out loud until your delivery is fluid. A conversational delivery (even with a few hiccups) will be a better fit for a party than the reading of a script.

BE CONCISE

Think Hemmingway, not Faulkner. Toasts should be short; one to two minutes is appropriate. If you are a special guest, like the host, best man, or matron of honor, you can stretch it to three or four minutes.

EXPLAIN YOUR CONNECTION

It doesn't have to be your opening line, but at an early point in your toast, describe your relationship to the guest(s) of honor.

HAVE A THEME

Every great speech has a hook. Toasts are no exception. You might simply have a theme that is then supported by a story or a few short anecdotes about the guest(s) of honor. Also consider starting with an inspirational quotation or passage and relating it to the guest(s) of honor. If you are comfortable using humor, start with a tasteful and topical joke and then provide a moral or advice that relates to the guest(s) of honor.

A wonderful example of a toast that opens with a catchy theme comes from the 2001 movie, *My First Mister*. The main character, Jennifer, a 17-year old girl, begins a toast with the line, "I'd like to propose a toast to all the special 'f' words—to friends, family, fate, forgiveness, and forever." It's funny, sincere, memorable, and masterfully sets up the rest of the toast.

AVOID INSIDER INFORMATION

When in doubt, leave it out. If it isn't possible or appropriate to explain a story or joke so that every guest can understand it, then it has no place in a toast. Leave that for a personal conversation or correspondence.

REMEMBER YOUR THANK YOUS

When giving a toast at a special event, think ahead to identify all the people you should thank or otherwise recognize. It could be the host(s), attendees, guest(s) of honor, or others who made the event possible. Don't miss out on an opportunity to show your gratitude publicly.

SAY "CHEERS!"

A toast is just a speech if there's no drink at the end. Don't forget to invite other guests to join you in toasting the guest(s) of honor. You can say, "Please join me in raising a glass to . . ." Or it can be as simple as, "Cheers!"

DELIVERING A SMOOTH TOAST

Now that you've done the legwork on the content of your toast, don't forget these simple tips to ensure the delivery goes smoothly:

LET THE HOST GO FIRST

Etiquette requires the host to give the first toast. You might be anxious to deliver your toast so you can get on with celebrating, but wait for the host to kick things off.

SPEAK BEFORE YOUR SECOND DRINK

On the subject of getting to celebrate, make sure you give your toast before you start your second drink. It might seem like a good idea to have a few drinks to calm your nerves, but it's not. Alcohol and public speaking don't mix well. Save yourself, the host, and guest(s) of honor potential embarrassment by sticking to water or speaking before you move on to your second adult drink.

HOLD THE MICROPHONE PROPERLY

Watch for the placement of the microphone when you give your toast. Hold it right up to your lips and you'll get a muffled or garbled sound, rather than a clear, amplified voice. Hold it too low or too far in front of you, and it won't pick up your voice.

Keep your chin up, speak with a strong voice, and hold the microphone at a 45 degree angle about four inches from your mouth (this is where you would hold an ice cream cone between licks). Avoid moving your hand on the microphone, as it can cause a distracting sound or even turn the microphone switch off. If you can, arrive at the celebration early and ask the event organizer for a moment to test out the microphone. You might also discuss details of when toasts will be given and where speakers should stand to avoid unpleasant feedback.

There will be plenty of opportunities to say a few words at special life events like weddings, anniversaries, graduations, and birthdays. Seize the opportunity to add to these important and joyous occasions.

EXERCISE

Craft a one to two minute toast that you could give at the retirement of a favorite mentor, boss, or teacher. Remember to describe your connection to the person you are speaking about, share the person's admirable characteristics (your theme), share an anecdote that exemplifies those qualities, thank the person for the impact he or she had on your life, and raise your glass in a toast. Rehearse and deliver the toast, aiming to speak with no notes or with a limited outline on a small notecard.

ACTIVITY

Watch and analyze a toast given at a special occasion—it can be one that you witnessed in person, saw in a movie, or found on YouTube. What was the speaker's theme? How was it supported? How could the toast have been more thoughtful, memorable, or appropriate? ▪

—— CHAPTER 36 ——

WHERE YOU SAY IT
Speeches to Inspire

In the film *Remember the Titans*, Coach Herman Boone (played by Denzel Washington) delivers a rousing speech in an attempt to unite his racially divided high school football team. Washington is a highly regarded actor who has won Academy Awards for both Best Actor (2001) and Best Supporting Actor (1989), and in that onscreen speech, we can see why.

Delivering a motivational speech in the real world is not quite the same. We are not Denzel Washington, nor do we get the benefit of multiple takes. It would be a mistake to try to reproduce the inspirational speeches from films like *Remember the Titans, Hoosiers, Braveheart,* or *Invictus.* How then, can we mere mortals craft inspirational speeches that can move listeners?

Because persuasion often is a secondary purpose of inspirational speeches, start by reviewing chapter 25 on persuading. In addition, consider the following advice for inspirational speaking:

BE AUTHENTIC

It is somewhat odd to say, "Be yourself" when discussing the act of public speaking. For most people, being yourself would include not giving public speeches! That said, it is important to avoid acting like someone else. Don't play a character; audiences recognize when you are disingenuous.

MAKE THE SENTIMENT CLEAR

Like all ceremonial speeches, it is important that a speech to inspire is sentimentally definitive. This means that if your purpose is to inspire, then the speech should avoid too much discussion of challenges or negativity. Also, have a clear point. Listeners should leave with a moral like "family is important," or "hard work will pay off." Your main idea need not be as specific or as explicitly stated as it would be in a how-to speech, training program, or sales pitch, but it must be present and conveyed to listeners.

BUILD TO YOUR POINT

An inspirational speech does not need to reach saccharine highs, but it does need to build toward a point. In doing this, you can certainly discuss challenges and hardships. Generally, discussion of obstacles is best placed at either the beginning or the middle of the presentation: if placed at the beginning, you can build toward the inspirational point; if placed in the middle, you are able to begin and end on more positive notes.

STYLISTIC DEVICES TO MOVE YOUR AUDIENCE

There are a number of stylistic devices that you can consider incorporating to help move your audience. Here are a few:

Isocolon is a scheme of parallel structure that occurs when the parallel elements are similar not only in grammatical structure but also in length (number of words, or even number, or syllables).

> Example: His purpose was to impress the ignorant, to perplex the dubious, and to confound the scrupulous.

Antithesis is the juxtaposition of contrasting ideas, often in parallel structure. The contrast may be in words or in ideas or both

> Example: What if I am rich, and another is poor; strong, and he is weak; intelligent, and he is benighted; elevated, and he is depraved? Have we not one Father? Hath not one God created us? – William Lloyd Garrison, "No Compromise with Slavery."

Anaphora is the repetition of the same word or groups of words at the beginnings of successive clauses. This device produces a strong emotional effect, especially in speech. It also establishes a marked change in rhythm.

> Example: Why should white people be running all the stores in our community? Why should white people be running the banks of our community? Why should the economy of our community be in the hands of the white man? Why? – Malcolm X.

Climax is the arrangement of words, phrases, or clauses in an order of increasing importance.

> Example: More than that, we rejoice in our sufferings, knowing that suffering produces endurance, endurance produces character, and character produces hope, and hope does not disappoint us, because God's love has been poured into our hearts through the Holy Spirit which has been given to us. – Paul to the Romans.

STYLISTIC DEVICES TO MOVE YOUR AUDIENCE (continued)

Chiasmus is the repetition of words in successive clauses in reverse syntactic order.

> Example: Ask not what your country can do for you; ask what you can do for your country. – John F. Kennedy, Inaugural address.

Atanaclasis is the repetition of a word in two different senses.

> Example: Your argument is sound, nothing but sound. – Benjamin Franklin.

> If we don't hang together, we'll hang separately. – Benjamin Franklin.

Hyperbole is exaggeration for the purpose of emphasis or heightened effect.

> Example: I nearly died I was so embarrassed.

Litotes is the deliberate use of understatement.

> Example: It isn't very serious. I have this tiny little tumor on the brain. – JD Salinger, The Catcher in the Rye

Paradox is apparently contradictory statement that nevertheless contains some measure of truth.

> Example: Art is a form of lying in order to tell the truth. – Pablo Picasso

Paralepsis is emphasizing something by seemingly passing over it.

> Example: I refuse to talk about my opponents multiple failed marriages. That is not what this campaign is about.

Hypophora is asking questions then immediately answering them.

> Example: Can we provide better service? Yes. Can we save you money? Yes. Will you become a member of ABC Credit Union? We hope you say yes.

TELL STORIES

Inspirational speakers often rely on stories, rather than facts or statistics, to support their message. Just make sure that you, the presenter, aren't always the hero in the stories told. True, personal narratives can lend credibility and increase rapport with listeners. But taken to the extreme, they can have the opposite effect and come across as self-congratulatory. In her book *Resonate*, Nancy Duarte uses a *Star Wars* metaphor and recommends that speakers leverage stories that put themselves in the Yoda/adviser role and cast audience members in the Luke Skywalker/hero role.

INVOLVE YOUR AUDIENCE

Inspiring an audience involves moving an audience. They might be moved to act or moved to think, but you are trying to move them. To that end, you should make explicit appeals to audience members (most often in the conclusion of an inspiration speech). Concretely describe how listeners achieve the principles or goals you discuss. Make sure this question does not go unanswered, else your motivational message will fall flat.

CLINCH CONFIDENTLY

Clinching speeches is always important. But it is even more important for a speech where your intent is to motivate. Without a confident ending, all of the hard work that you have done in the speech will be minimized. (See chapter 20 for more on effective clinchers.)

Inspirational speeches are part persuasion, part ceremonial speech. Considering the above factors will help you find the right balance for your specific purpose, audience, and context.

EXERCISE

After you have written an inspirational speech, re-read it and answer the following questions: What points do I want to build toward? Have I highlighted those points with the language I've chosen? If the answer to either is no then revise the speech with attention to using your language and, perhaps a rhetorical device, to elevate your point.

ACTIVITY

Watch and analyze an inspirational speech from a movie that you have seen or from one of those listed at the beginning of this chapter. What was the speaker's point? How did he or she build up to it? What did the speech move listeners to do? Why was it effective for the audience? How could it have been better? ▪

—————— CHAPTER 37 ——————

WHERE YOU SAY IT
After Dinner Speaking

Every year, the White House Correspondents' Association (WHCA) holds a dinner at which the president of the United States is the guest of honor. Started in 1920, these dinners began as rather small affairs. Now, the occasion attracts not just the president and members of the White House Press Corps, but celebrities from television, film, music, and sports. The event has always been an occasion studded with entertainment, the highlight of which has become a series of after dinner speeches delivered by an invited performer—usually a comedian—and a response by the president. Notable performers at the WHCA Dinner have included Richard Pryor, Jay Leno, Stephen Colbert, Conan O'Brien, and Wanda Sykes.

In general, after dinner speeches are meant to entertain. Consider the context indicated by the name of this type of presentation: Audience members have just finished eating and likely are still enjoying spirits. They are satiated and more relaxed than when the meal began. Given those factors, attempts to persuade the audience to remove the salary cap from professional football or informing the audience about new governmental guidelines for accountants would seem ill advised. The occasion is not amenable to those ends. What should you be considering for an after dinner speech?

THE SENTIMENT SHOULD BE LIGHT HEARTED

As you consider what to write, don't burden yourself with trying to be profound or deeply moving. Have a point, and perhaps even a persuasive one, but keep it light.

BE ENTERTAINING IN A WAY THAT MAKES SENSE TO YOU

Many after dinner speeches are humorous, but don't feel like you must play the role of a comedian. Entertainment can happen with stories, anecdotes, hypotheticals, and vivid description. It does not have to be jokes. And if you do tell jokes, be mindful of their appropriateness. It is easy to get caught up in the moment—everyone seems relaxed and is having a good time, so you decide to push the boundary and tell an embarrassing story about a co-worker or an off-color joke. Just remember, you can't take it back once you say it. Also, no one ever got fired for not telling a joke, but plenty of people have experienced the negative repercussions of being inappropriate.

THE STRUCTURE OF AN AFTER DINNER SPEECH CAN BE SUBTLE

Your goal for this speech is to contribute to the mood more than it is to persuade listeners to your position or to inform audience members about a specific topic. Because data retention is not a primary goal, after dinner speeches often have subtle previews and transitions in place of the more direct signposting that you would use in an informative briefing or persuasive presentation.

DON'T EXPECT AN ATTENTIVE AUDIENCE

Audience members may be finishing their meal, finding the restroom, or even conversing with nearby dining mates. If you are in a banquet room, you will be speaking over servers clearing plates, refilling drinks, and generally circulating throughout the room. Don't allow the distractions to frustrate you. Expect them; they are just part of the context.

Also, in your preparation, include a few clear statements that express the sentiment you are trying to achieve. Repetition, directness, and simplicity will help ensure listeners get the main idea despite the distractions.

After dinner speeches and dessert share many characteristics. They both mark the end of the meal, they both should be enjoyable, and you should avoid having too much of either. If you understand the expectations for the occasion and play to your own strengths, your speech, much like an excellent dessert, will be delightful.

EXERCISE

In preparation for an after dinner speech, practice your presentation with the television on. If you can remain focused while managing visual and aural distractions, you will be better able to handle disruptions from the audience.

ACTIVITY

Watch Stephen Colbert's White House Correspondents' Dinner speech (www.youtube.com/watch?v=U7FTF4Oz4dI).

Is the speech sentimentally definitive? Who is Colbert's audience—the audience in the room or some larger audience? How did Colbert negotiate the distractions that come with after dinner speaking? What are strengths of his speech? How could it have been better? ▪

──────── CHAPTER 38 ────────

WHERE YOU SAY IT
Unexpected Places to Gain Speaking Experience

You don't need to give a lectern-style speech or lead a meeting at work to focus on developing your presentation skills. In fact, presenting in situations outside the office can help you build confidence so you can ace your next workplace presentation.

Here are some unexpected places where you can hone your presentation skills:

STORES AND RESTAURANTS

Ordering food at a restaurant or coffee shop is a great way to work on your voice. Because such settings are very often are noisy, you have the opportunity to speak loudly and get comfortable using a booming voice. And you also are well served to practice speaking slowly, clearly and concisely when you are ordering, asking a question, or describing something you are looking for.

SOCIAL EVENTS

Happy hours and networking events are fantastic places to train yourself to smile and to hone your listening skills. After all, when you are meeting old friends and making new acquaintances, keeping a smile on your face will help you appear welcoming and interested. After a few hours in these social situations, your face should feel tired from all the smiling.

Additionally, your ears may be ringing from all the listening you have done. Many professionals make the mistake of going to networking events to talk about themselves. Instead, you should go to networking events to listen. Turn your focus to getting the people you meet to open up.

And don't forget social gatherings such as weddings, anniversary parties, graduations, and holiday celebrations. These special occasions are precious opportunities to tell the people we love how much we care about them. Consider giving a toast at such event and developing your abilities to craft a well-structured speech, share thoughtful anecdotes, and even present without notes.

HOUSES OF WORSHIP

Temples, churches, mosques, and other places of worship can provide opportunities to develop your presentation skills. If passages from religious texts are read aloud by lay people during service where you worship, volunteer to be a reader. This is a great way to learn to manage nervous energy, to speak slowly and clearly, to improve vocal inflection, and to master the manuscript mode of public speaking.

Additionally, many houses of worship have youth education programs. Serving as a teacher in this capacity can help you structure programs with a clear central idea and objectives, plan active learning exercises, as well as respond off the cuff to difficult questions.

NON-PROFIT ORGANIZATIONS

If you associate with a non-profit or service organization, consider volunteering in ways that advance the goals of the organization and your speaking skills at the same time.

Similar to religious education opportunities, training programs offered to staff or clients of non-profits can improve your ability to structure presentations, manage time (especially when you incorporate hands-on exercises), and shine during Q&A sessions. Additionally, consider serving as an emcee at a fundraising event to develop your ability to manage nervousness, use a microphone, transition from one part of a program to another, and introduce speakers effectively.

And don't overlook the learning that occurs when you work a phone bank, information booth, or doorbelling operation. These activities will encourage you to smile, build rapport quickly, speak concisely, and help you develop thick skin.

LOCAL SCHOOLS

There are myriad opportunities to develop your speaking skills while you engage with students in your area. And don't worry if you don't have school-age kids—educational institutions welcome involvement from all community members.

For elementary schools, there may be opportunities to read aloud in classrooms. This will help you speak loudly and slowly, as well as tell stories dramatically by adding vocal variations and hand gestures. For older students, you might be able to gain experience speaking to larger groups at a career-day event or even as a guest speaker at an assembly. Or perhaps you can hone listening skills by serving as a mentor.

You may even find opportunities to present to college students in your area or at your alma mater. Many professors welcome practitioners in the field to guest lecture, and career development offices will often tap local professionals or alumni for career fairs, panel discussions, and roundtables.

ON STAGE

Though qualitatively different than public speaking, performing on stage can help you develop skills for managing nervousness and presenting with confidence. Consider auditioning to perform at your local little theatre, storytelling corps, improv group, or poetry competition.

Remember, you don't need to deliver a keynote address or facilitate your company's annual meeting to advance your presentation skills. Embrace opportunities to build your confidence and speak with authority when you are shopping, socializing, worshipping, and volunteering.

EXERCISE

Identify three unexpected place to gain experience as a speaker that would advance presentation skills that you would like to improve. Research options in your community. Select one based on your goals as a presenter and the opportunities available to you; make arrangements to speak there.

ACTIVITY

Think of a time when you spoke at one of the aforementioned unexpected places to gain experience as a speaker. What principles of effective public speaking could you have applied in that situation to improve your effectiveness/performance? How will you approach speaking in this context differently in the future? ▪

——— CHAPTER 39 ———

WHAT NEXT
Concluding Remarks and How to Continue Improving

The introduction of this handbook referenced the refined presentation skills of former U.S. President Bill Clinton and Apple co-founder and CEO Steve Jobs, both noteworthy leaders who articulated their ideas effectively and changed the world in which they lived. These leaders didn't take a crash course in public speaking during the days, weeks, or months leading up to their moment in the spotlight—they relied on years of experience and a longtime commitment to excellence in public speaking.

LEARNING TO SPEAK WITH AUTHORITY WILL PROPEL YOU TO POSITIONS OF LEADERSHIP, ADVANCE YOUR CAREER, AND LEND VOICE TO YOUR IDEAS FOR SOLVING PRESSING PROBLEMS IN OUR WORLD.

At the conclusion of this handbook, it is our hope that you too make a career-long, if not lifelong, commitment to honing your presentation skills and that you take action today to develop those skills. Learning to speak with authority will propel you to positions of leadership, advance your career, and lend voice to your ideas for solving pressing problems in our world (even if you don't aspire to become the president of the United States or the CEO of a company).

By reading to this point in the text, you have, at the very least, learned some basics of what you say (presentation content), how you say it (presentation delivery), and where you say it (tips on presenting in specific workplace contexts). And by utilizing this handbook in conjunction with the exercises and activities at the end of each chapter or as a supplement to a formal class or training program, you will be even further along in your development as a speaker.

But, please, don't stop here. Rather than viewing the last chapter of this handbook as an endpoint, consider it the end of the beginning of your journey toward excellence as a presenter. You might be wondering then, "How can I continue on this path toward excellence and maintained the momentum I already have built?"

First and foremost: seek out opportunities to speak. Speak up in meetings; ask questions after lectures, briefings, and conference proceedings; participate in panel discussions; conduct training programs; land keynote roles at conferences; and, give toasts at special life events. (See chapter 38 for ideas on unexpected places to gain experience as a speaker.)

Additionally, consider opportunities to take your presentation skills to the next level in the following three ways:

ENROLL IN A CLASS

If you were introduced to this handbook through a class you are enrolled in, congratulations! Consider enrolling in an advanced presentation-skills course.

If you haven't already taken a course in public speaking—and many well-educated professionals have not—sign up for one. Colleges and universities are a great resource for undergraduate and graduate students, but many also accommodate professionals who want to take a class for no credit or who want to earn a certificate in a communication-related specialty.

Another option for professionals is to find a class that is not affiliated with a college or university. The Dale Carnegie program is a well-known and intensive presentation-skills course for professionals. But there are many others. Check with local community centers, professional associations, and even your human resources department at work to see what is available in your area.

When considering enrolling in a class, make sure the class size is small enough to afford you ample opportunities to practice and receive feedback (25 participants or fewer for break-out practice sessions is a good rule of thumb). After all, you can't learn how to become an excellent speaker passively; you have to gain experience speaking to improve. Enrolling in a participatory class can give you an intensive dose of instruction and practice over the course of a few days, weeks, or months that can catapult your presentation skills to the next level.

JOIN A CLUB

Toastmasters International is the most widely known association of clubs that are dedicated to helping members improve their public speaking skills. With around 300,000 members in clubs spanning the globe, Toastmasters clubs generally meet on a weekly or semi-monthly basis and follow a standard meeting format. The one-hour meeting format consists of three segments: first, members give prepared speeches based on objectives explained in educational materials provided by Toastmasters International; second, meeting participants respond to questions posed by the so-call Table Topics Master to gain experience with off-the-cuff speaking; and lastly, prepared speakers receive oral and written feedback from a fellow club member on the speech they delivered at the beginning of the meeting.

The main benefit of joining a Toastmasters Club is building public speaking into your long-term schedule. This allows you to learn new presentation skills and make them habit, to gain experience and build confidence speaking in a low-risk and friendly environment, to help maintain your motivation to develop as a public speaker, and to prevent the atrophy of your oral communication abilities between important workplace presentations.

Additionally, membership to Toastmasters International offers opportunities to compete in public speaking competitions and to serve as a leader within the volunteer-run organization. Long-term and active membership in a Toastmasters club also can enhance your social and professional network. Compared to other presentation skills training opportunities, a Toastmasters membership falls at a relatively low price point. When considering a club to join, visit several that are convenient to your home or work. Each chapter has its own feel; invest in finding a group that has strong evaluators and that is a good personality match for you.

HIRE A COACH

The benefit of hiring a coach is getting one-on-one attention so you can ace a make-or-break presentation. Make-or-break presentations can catapult your career—think job interviews, performance reviews that determine promotions, and important pitches to investors or clients; they can bolster your position as a thought leader in your area of expertise—think commencement speeches, keynote addresses, and panel presentations; and they can provide an opportunity to tell the people you love how much you care about them—think toasts and eulogies.

Though one-on-one instruction will almost certainly be more expensive than enrolling in a class or joining a club, it stands to provide the biggest breakthrough in your presentation skills (and thus makes sense to do for the most important speaking occasions). Make sure to make the most of your investment by selecting a good coach.

There is no industry certification for public speaking coaches, but the person you select as your coach should:

- Have a track record of helping professionals succeed in the speaking genre you are focusing on;

- Have an expertise in communication (either by education, training, experience, or a combination thereof);

- Have a published list of clients and satisfied references who you can contact;

- Focus on both the content and delivery of your presentation, but do so in a way as to help you find and refine your authentic voice (and not to blindly follow conventions that aren't consistent with your style or personality);

- Provide suggestions not only for the specific presentation you are working on, but advice and systems that you can apply to other speaking situations;

- Review video recordings of practice speeches with you to point out strengths and areas to improve;

- Encourage and motivate you, but also push you past your comfort zone so you can achieve major breakthroughs in your presentation skills.

	Phase in Career	Speaking Needs	Price Point
Class	Ideal for early career and mid-career professionals who struggle with public speaking	Learning new skills and best practices Getting practice	$$
Club	Useful for any career stage, ideal for early career	Making newly learned skills habit Gaining experience and building confidence	$
Coach	Ideal for mid- and late-career professionals, advisable for job seekers in any career stage	Capitalizing on make-or-break speaking opportunities like keynote addresses, pitches to key stakeholders, and job/promotion interviews	$$$

$ | $75-$300 a year
$$ | $200-$5,000 a class depending on class size, number of meetings, intensity, and reputation of the program
$$$ | $150-$500+ an hour

Whether through a class, club, or coach, we urge you to continue developing your presentation skills throughout your career. Because, as we hope you now are convinced, strong communication skills always are in demand.

It is our sincere hope that this text will serve as a useful guide on your journey toward excellence as a presenter. Keep it close at hand to remind you of best practices and as a resource when you find yourself presenting in new or nerve-racking situations. Congratulations and good luck on your quest to find your authentic voice, to unlock your potential, and to change the world by speaking with authority. ▪

———— APPENDIX ————

ONE
Sample Outlines for Various Occasions

EXAMPLE / BRIEFING

Overview of ABC Project
Preview

| T | I. Phase One | T | II. Phase Two |

    I. Phase One   II. Phase Two

    A.   A.

    B.   B.

    C.   C.

    D.   D.

Review

EXAMPLE / ACADEMIC RESEARCH

Thesis of Paper
Preview

| T | I. Context/Importance | T | II. Research Methods | T | III. Conclusions |

    A.   A.   A.

    B.   B.   B.

    C.   C.   C.

Future Research
Review

EXAMPLE / PITCH

Attention
Adopt XYZ Strategy **Preview**

T   I. Need
     (Problem)
	T II. Satisfaction
	     (Solution)
		T III. Visualization
		     (Benefits)

A.	A.	A.
B.	B.	B.
C.	C.	C.

Review
Call to Action

EXAMPLE / MEETING

Decide on a Vendor **Preview**

T I. Vendor A	T II. Vendor B	T III. Vendor C
A.	A.	A.
B.	B.	B.
C.	C.	C.

Vote **Next Steps**

EXAMPLE / Q & A

Restate/Rephrase Question
Your Position **Preview**
[T] I. Reason One   [T] II. Reason Two
Review
Restate Position

EXAMPLE / PANEL PRESENTATION

Theme of Panel **Preview**
[T] I. Speaker 1   [T] II. Speaker 2   [T] III. Speaker 3   [T] IV. Speaker 4
Q & A Session **Review**

EXAMPLE / TOAST

Theme Relating to Couple **Preview**
[T] I. Anecdote One   [T] II. Anecdote Two
Review

———— APPENDIX ————

TWO
Recover from a Disappointing Presentation

High-school senior Morgan McCauley was elated to learn she would be the recipient of a prestigious and selective National Honor Society leadership award. But elation soon turned to terror when she found out she would have to give an acceptance speech to an assembly of her teachers, classmates, and their families.

Despite carefully scripting and practicing her speech, things went from bad to worse when she was introduced at the event. Wearing an air cast for a sprained ankle, Morgan tripped as she left her seat. Then, she fell on the stairs leading from the podium to the lectern. When she finally got to the lectern, Morgan looked up at the crowd before her and mumbled, "Oh my gosh, there so many people here." It was picked up in the microphone; she started to cry. After several minutes of crying, an English teacher joined Morgan at the lectern, took her script, and read the speech, all while Morgan stood there in tears.

Perhaps you have had an experience like Morgan, which she described as "scarring." But even if not (and hopefully you haven't), you likely can empathize with the experience of giving a disappointing presentation—one that did not go as well as you had hoped or one that you weren't proud of. What, then, can you do to recover from a bad presentation and to prevent the experience from eroding your confidence?

PUT IT IN PERSPECTIVE

As embarrassing or deflating as it can be, giving a bad speech is nothing more than an off performance. It doesn't mean you are a bad person, a terrible speaker, a subpar student or employee, (insert your own putdown here). After all, bad speeches happen to good people. Remember to keep things in perspective and separate the person from the performance.

ANALYZE WHAT WENT WRONG . . . AND RIGHT

If you need to, wallow in disappointment for a day or two. Then, focus on studying what happened during your presentation so you can learn from the experience.

As difficult as it will be, and no matter how strong the temptation to avoid thinking about the speech again, examine evidence to identify what went wrong. Lisa Braithwaite, a public speaking trainer and coach from Santa Barbara, Calif., encouraged speakers to review video or audio, "It's easier to analyze when you watch or listen, than to trust your memory. We tend to blow mistakes out of proportion and to be really hard on ourselves. It's hard to look objectively."

But don't stop with your analysis of what went wrong. "When we get down on ourselves, we need to remember what went right," continued Braithwaite. "Look at the presentation and realize that a lot went well. Find the high notes and remember to do that next time." If there is no recording of the speech, look to session evaluations or solicit feedback from a neutral audience member to conduct your analysis of what went wrong and right.

Also, be specific with your observations. Rather than noting the general use of filler words, identify what fillers you used ("uh"), how many times you used them (24 times), in what context they were used (at the beginning of sentences), and how the behavior impacted your presentation (e.g., made me look unprofessional and like I didn't know my material). The more detail you include, the more successful you will be with your plans for improving.

TROUBLESHOOT

After you identify what went wrong, analyze why it went wrong. In a personal interview with Susan Trivers, an executive speaking coach, she said that a lack of preparation is often to blame. She urged speakers to give an honest assessment, "Ask yourself, really, how much time did I spend preparing? Try to quantify it."

Other times you will find psychological or situational factors at the root of the problem. Perhaps you were intimidated by speaking to such a large group, you were distracted by a personal problem, you didn't get a good night's sleep, you didn't eat breakfast, you were coming down with a cold, or you were running late for the presentation.

CRAFT A PLAN

After you identify all the factors that contributed to a lackluster performance, come up with specific strategies to prevent them from recurring. Rather than saying you will better analyze the audience, define exactly what that means. For example, you could resolve to:

- Read the organization's website, especially material pertaining to the mission, recent work, and conference at which you are presenting, at least two months before the presentation;

- Research recent news accounts of the organization and key members at least two months before the presentation;

- Have a conversation with the event organizer at least two months before the presentation;

- Talk to at least four rank-and-file audience members about their needs and interests at least six weeks before the presentation;

- And, craft the thesis and main points of your presentation based on your analysis of the audience, at least a month before the presentation.

Specificity is crucial. Identify what your plan for improvement entails and when you will complete each component of it for your next presentation. Each item should be actionable and time limited.

GET BACK ON STAGE

Now that you have identified what when wrong, why it happened, and how you will prevent similar problems, it's time to heed the advice offered in this old saw: when you fall off the horse, get right back in the saddle. Don't allow a bad experience to paralyze you with fear. The best way to prevent that is to run, not walk, to the stage for your next speech.

It is not necessary for you to repeat the same type of presentation or speaking situation right away. If you bombed a keynote address, consider speaking on a panel for an upcoming conference. And don't overlook other opportunities in your professional or personal life to speak in public again, such as: providing a speech of introduction at a conference, giving a toast, or reading a passage of Scripture at church.

The goal is to rebuild your confidence as a speaker. It may take a series of baby steps to get back to delivering featured speeches. That's okay. What is important is that you start taking steps and making progress within a few weeks of your disappointing presentation. The longer you wait, the steeper the climb.

MEASURE PROGRESS

After every presentation, track your progress. Be proactive in recording speeches and getting feedback, whenever appropriate. Figure out where your plans for preventing lackluster performances worked, and where you can and should modify them.

Seeing evidence of improvement will be a boon to your confidence. Carefully reviewing presentations will also allow you to identify areas you still need to work on, helping you become an even better speaker.

CONSIDER A COACH

When recovering from a bad presentation, consider hiring a speech coach to help you through some or all of the recovery process.

"People focus on climbing the career ladder by getting a master's degree or certification in their area, but then rely on speaking skills they learned in one class as an undergraduate," lamented Trivers during the same personal interview, "Don't rely on outdated presentation skills training. Coaches hone our craft all the time. We are constantly at the forefront of what works with audiences—we bring that outside perspective."

Think about it in terms of any other expert you hire to improve your professional image, like those who cut hair, tailor suits, shine and repair shoes, or write resumes. It is just as important, if not more important, to invest in an expert who can help you feel proud of your speeches and project more confidence every time you communicate in your professional and personal life.

BELIEVE IN COMEBACKS

If you are nursing a few wounds after delivering an off speech, it is possible to recover from a disappointing performance, or a disastrous speech like Morgan's. After the traumatic experience at her high school awards assembly, Morgan went on to earn her undergraduate degree from Wesleyan University, where she struggled through required class presentations.

In the fall of 2012, Morgan began her professional career as a legal assistant at a large law firm in Washington, D.C. She completed a small-group public speaking class to improve her confidence as a speaker. "I'm a little more comfortable, especially in small groups, but I still get freaked out by the idea of speaking to big groups," admitted Morgan. With additional experience and effort, she surely will find her voice and speak with authority even before large audiences.

EXERCISE

Recall a disappointing or devastating speaking experience. Why do you think it went poorly? What could you have done differently to prevent the lackluster performance? How will you approach future speeches differently?

ACTIVITY

If presentations will be a part of your life, it is a good idea to keep notes on how you perform. Much of the research in educational psychology notes that the lessons learned from speaking and writing are not retained unless there is some reflection on those experiences.

Keeping a file on your desktop or easily accessible through cloud computing can allow you to quickly jot down things that don't work and things that do. It is also a great place to collect ideas from other presentations that you see. Having reflected on the moment, it is more likely that you will recall the lesson and be able to use it whenever the occasion presents itself. ▪

—————— APPENDIX ——————

THREE
Impromptu Speech Topics

TOPICS FOR INFORMATIVE SPEAKING

1. Describe how to make your favorite dish.

2. Describe two highlights from a vacation you have taken.

3. Describe a useful shortcut you have discovered.

4. Describe the history of a tradition to which you adhere.

5. Describe a skill you learned at work.

6. Describe the biography of a person you admire.

7. Describe the steps you took to accomplish a long-term goal.

8. Describe something you do to maintain good health.

9. Describe a way that you have saved money.

10. Describe a little-known resource in your community.

TOPICS FOR PERSUASIVE SPEAKING

1. Pitch a book that you think we should read.

2. Tell us about a product we should buy today.

3. What off-the-beaten-path attraction should every tourist to your hometown visit?

4. What is the best local restaurant?

5. What useful course should every high school or college student take?

6. Tell us why we should watch your favorite movie or TV show.

7. Persuade us to take up a new hobby or activity.

8. Convince us to reject a commonly accepted practice.

9. Extol the virtues of disconnecting from a specific technology.

10. What frivolous expense do you think is worth splurging on?

TOPICS FOR DEBATES

1. Online education—boom or bust?

2. Does e-mail help or hinder interpersonal relationships?

3. Do smartphones keep people connected or distracted?

4. Blogs—worthless or worthwhile?

5. Is technology widening or closing the gap between socio-economic classes?

6. Is it ethical or unethical for corporate leaders to deliver speeches written by speechwriters as if the speeches were their own words and thoughts?

7. Should college professors grade group work individually or collectively?

8. Playing video games—a brain drain or brain builder?

9. Does television programming celebrate or suppress alternative voices?

10. Does text messaging promote direct communication or miscommunication?

TOPICS FOR JOB INTERVIEWS

1. Describe your ideal supervisor.

2. Where do you want to be in your career in five years?

3. Are you better working in teams or individually?

4. What did you like least about your last job?

5. What is your greatest weakness/strength?

6. What two adjectives would your supervisor use to describe you?

7. Describe the accomplishment for which you are the most proud.

8. Describe someone who has had a positive influence on your career.

9. How do you keep yourself organized?

10. What do you like to do for fun?

TOPICS FOR STORYTELLING

1. Describe a risk you have taken that turned out successfully.

2. Describe your first or worst job.

3. Describe a time that you took the road less traveled.

4. Describe a time when your vacation turned into a trip from hell.

5. Describe a time when you were blamed for something you didn't do.

6. Describe the most exciting day in your life.

7. Describe an event you attended that was more fun than you expected.

8. Describe a time when your assumption was wrong.

9. Describe your most memorable holiday or celebration.

10. Describe an experience that changed your worldview.

EXERCISE

Select a letter and give a speech inspired by the word that begins with that letter.

airplane	nurse
bakery	orange
camouflage	pillow
dentist	quiz
exercise	rope
Ferris wheel	soccer
guacamole	toddler
harmonica	utopia
invisible	vaccine
juvenile	watermelon
kitchen	x-ray
lighthouse	yoga
microphone	zero

——— APPENDIX ———

FOUR
Annotated List of Useful Websites for Public Speakers

American Rhetoric | www.americanrhetoric.com

Have you ever watched in its entirety Dr. Martin Luther King Jr.'s famous "I Have a Dream" speech? What about former President Ronald Reagan's "Challenger" address after the space shuttle's tragic accident in 1986? These and other famous examples of American public address are catalogued at the American Rhetoric website by Professors Stephen Lucas and Martin Medhurst. It is an invaluable resource for speakers who strive to understand how to make appeals that can impact listeners and change the world.

Dale Carnegie Training | www.dalecarnegie.com

In 1912, Dale Carnegie offered his first public speaking course at a YMCA in New York. Over 100 years later, his legacy as a leader in self-improvement training endures. The Dale Carnegie Training website now offers a range of books, seminars, courses, online trainings, and events on presentation effectiveness, sales, leadership, as well as other topics geared toward contemporary business professionals.

Nancy Duarte | www.duarte.com

Known for authoring award-winning books *Resonate: Present Visual Stories that Transform Audiences* and *Slide:ology: The Art and Science of Creating Great Presentations*, Nancy Duarte explains on her website that she "applies storytelling and visual thinking principles to business communications that shift audience beliefs and behaviors." Her site offers speakers insights into her perspective on persuasion, information on accessing her publications, as well as a blog with presenting advice and event announcements.

National Communication Association | www.natcom.org

Want to find the most recent academic research on public speaking and other communication-related topics? Look first to the *Quarterly Journal of Speech, Communication Monographs,* and the *Journal of Applied Communication Research,* all official publications of the National Communication Association. The organization's website also contains links to articles and webinars aimed at "scholars, teachers, and practitioners" in the academic discipline of communication.

National Speakers Association | www.nsaspeaker.org

Are you interested in making a living as a paid speaker? With chapters across the United States, the National Speakers Association is the leading organization for professional speakers. Its website provides information about chapter meetings and conferences, which provide educational programming for members and aspiring-members alike.

Patricia Fripp | www.fripp.com/blog

Wearing the hats of both a professional speaker and a presentation-skills coach for executives, Patricia Fripp's blog is filled with material that is relevant to seasoned speakers and straightforward enough for novices. Many posts include her video instruction, offering students of public speaking an opportunity to see Fripp practice what she preaches.

Presentation Zen | www.presentationzen.com

Authored by Garr Reynolds, who wrote a popular and useful book by the same title that focuses on presentation design and delivery, *Presentation Zen* is a regularly updated blog that studious speakers should follow. Reynolds highlights effective presentations and analyzes why they work, often using video clips to illustrate his points.

Google Presentations | drive.google.com

Microsoft's PowerPoint dominates the market for presentation software; however, there are other options. One free option that resembles PowerPoint in form and function is Google Presentations. Google Presentations is part of Google Drive, which is a bundle of programs similar to Microsoft Office. Google Presentations can be used online or downloaded for offline use.

Prezi | www.prezi.com

An increasingly popular alternative to PowerPoint, Prezi provides speakers a virtual whiteboard to supplement presentations. The platform's signature "zoomable" canvas allows speakers a visual way to show listeners the connections between main ideas in a presentation, as well as the functionality of focusing in on details. (See more in chapter 21 on Prezi.) Users can sign up for a free account on the Prezi website; helpful tutorials, presentations templates, and sample Prezi's also are available.

Ragan | www.ragan.com

Promoted as providing "news and ideas for communicators," the Lawrence Ragan Communications, Inc., website caters to corporate communications professionals—in public relations, speechwriting, human resources, and organizational communications. The firm's free, content-rich newsletters have great advice on public speaking and communication that provide value to anyone interested in developing presentation skills. And for corporate communicators, Ragan's paid workshops and conferences are well respected in the industry.

Six Minutes | www.sixminutes.dlugan.com

Written by Andrew Dlugan, an engineer and seasoned member of Toastmasters International, Six Minutes is a presentation skills blog that offers a bounty of original content on topics ranging from effective speech delivery and presentation aids to reviews of public speaking books and analyses of noteworthy speeches. It is geared toward members of Toastmasters (as evidenced by the blog's name, which pays homage to the five to seven minute time window given for most prepared speeches delivered at Toastmasters clubs), but material on the site is relevant to any presenter interested in developing his or her skills.

Spoken with Authority | www.spokenwithauthority.com

Hosted by co-author of this book Christine Clapp, the Spoken with Authority website describes consulting services as well as catalogues educational articles and videos for speakers. Most importantly, the site provides a free online speech-planning tool that guides presenters as they utilize the Sandwich Structure (see chapter 11 for details) to craft and print outlines that encourage an engaging and conversational presentation delivery style.

TED | www.ted.com

Launched in 1984 as a conference exploring the intersection of technology, entertainment, and design, TED has flourished into a global community of thought leaders from all disciplines who aim to share new ideas, change attitudes, and as a result, improve the world. The non-profit organization is best known for providing innovators a platform (both literally and online) to present their ideas "usually in the form of short, powerful talks (18 minutes or less)," according to the TED website. The dynamic, engaging style of heralded TED Talks has for many become the standard by which 21st century public speakers are gauged.

Toastmasters International | www.toastmasters.org

Want to join a public speaking club to gain experience and build confidence as a presenter? Toastmasters International is world renowned for its global network of clubs that are committed to developing the communication and leadership skills of members. The organization's website has a "Find a Club" search tool so you can locate a chapter near you; it also is a fantastic resource for free educational articles and videos on public speaking.

Vital Speeches of the Day | www.vsotd.com

Founded as a magazine that publishes important, contemporary speeches in their entirety, *Vital Speeches of the Day* now also has a website that archives noteworthy speeches. Like American Rhetoric, it serves as a clearinghouse of exceptional addresses that are instructive to students of public address. But, Vital Speeches has more of an international focus; in fact, its mission is to "represent the best thoughts of the best minds on current national and international issues."

YouTube | www.youtube.com

This video-sharing site offers a way to find and watch recordings of presentations (among videos on many, many other subjects). More importantly for public speakers, YouTube provides users the ability to create a "channel" to aggregate recordings of their own presentations as well as the recordings of other speakers. This gives speakers a means of collecting videos privately for future reference and sharing them with selected viewers or even millions of other YouTube users.

——— APPENDIX ———

FIVE
Additional Resources on Presenting and Speechwriting

Carnegie, Dale. *How to Win Friends & Influence People*. New York: Simon and Schuster, 1942.

Duarte, Nancy. *Resonate: Present Visual Stories That Transform Audiences*. Hoboken, N.J.: Wiley, 2010.

Foer, Joshua. *Moonwalking with Einstein: The Art and Science of Remembering Everything*. New York: Penguin Books, 2011.

Heath, Chip, and Dan Heath. *Made to Stick: Why Some Ideas Survive and Others Die*. New York: Random House, 2007.

Heinrichs, Jay. *Thank You for Arguing: What Aristotle, Lincoln, and Homer Simpson Can Teach Us About the Art of Persuasion*. New York: Three Rivers Press, 2007.

Humes, James C. *Confessions of a White House Ghostwriter: Five Presidents and Other Political Adventures*. Washington, D.C.: Regnery Pub., 1997.

Lanham, Richard A. *A Handlist of Rhetorical Terms: A Guide for Students of English Literature*. Berkeley: University of California Press, 1968.

Lehrman, Robert. *The Political Speechwriters' Companion: A Guide for Writers and Speakers*. Washington: CQ Press, 2009.

Noonan, Peggy. *What I Saw at the Revolution: A Political Life in the Reagan Era*. New York: Random House, 1990.

Reid, Ronald F. and James F. Klumpp. *American Rhetorical Discourse*. 3rd ed. Long Grove, IL: Waveland Press. 2005.

Reynolds, Garr. *Presentation Zen: Simple Ideas on Presentation Design and Delivery*. 2nd ed. Berkeley, CA: New Riders, 2012.

Ritter, Kurt W., and Martin J Medhurst. *Presidential Speechwriting: From the New Deal to the Reagan Revolution and Beyond*. College Station: Texas A&M University Press, 2003.

Safire, William. *Lend Me Your Ears: Great Speeches in History*. Rev. and expanded ed. New York: W.W. Norton, 1997.

Schlesinger, Robert. *White House Ghosts: Presidents and Their Speechwriters*. New York: Simon & Schuster, 2008.

Sorensen, Theodore C. *Counselor: A Life at the Edge of History*. New York: Harper, 2008.

Wills, Garry. *Lincoln at Gettysburg: The Words That Remade America*. New York: Simon & Schuster, 1992.

──── ACKNOWLEDGEMENTS ────

At Willamette University, where Christine Clapp and Bjørn Stillion Southard both earned their undergraduate degrees in Rhetoric and Media Studies, the motto is: "Not unto ourselves alone are we born." It also is a fitting motto for this book. After all, the intention was to craft an easily accessible and practical text that serves readers who want to advance their career, solve pressing problems, fulfill their leadership potential, and leave a lasting legacy. Thank you for reading it and implementing the ideas herein to speak with authority and improve the world.

Even more importantly, the motto is apropos because it points to the fact that this book would not be possible without the support and help of many people to whom the authors owe a debt of gratitude.

A NOTE FROM CHRISTINE

I would like to start by thanking Bjorn Stillion Southard, my first debate partner at Willamette, for undertaking this book project with me. I couldn't ask for a better friend, colleague, and collaborator. (Robert Trapp, thanks for partnering us in the fall of 1998 and mentoring us ever since.)

Next, I need to thank my family for their support. Douglas Clapp, thank you for being an incredibly supportive spouse, most notably in 2008 when I first suggested leaving my job on Capitol Hill to pursue a presentation skills consultancy. I'm so glad that you didn't run the car off the road and that Spoken with Authority is thriving today. And to my children Finnian and Beatrix Clapp, thank you for reminding me everyday what is important.

I am also grateful for my parents, Karen and Neil Hanson, both educators and principled leaders. Among so many other things, you instilled in me a strong work ethic and love for learning. Beth Sparks, my older sister, I also credit you with laying a foundation for my academic and professional successes. Thanks for coming home from school when we were kids and teaching me what you were learning four grades ahead.

I also want to express my gratitude to several people who helped make this book a reality: Wm. R. "Mac" McKenney for providing thoughtful edits and insightful suggestions to draft chapters of this book and just about everything I write, Allie Benjamin for copyediting this text, and Melissa Tenpas for the cover and interior design.

Lastly, thanks to my clients and members of the Spoken with Authority community, students and colleagues at the George Washington University, and fellow Toastmasters who helped me refine many of the ideas articulated in this book and encouraged me to publish them.

A NOTE FROM BJØRN

The first thank you is to Christine Clapp. Not once in the time that we were debate partners, Rhetoric majors at Willamette, MA students at Maryland, or co-authors of this book did we argue about either of us shirking our duties. We've always just seemed to work. No doubt Robert knew this.

The second thank you is to my family. Belinda, Ella, and Finna have supported this project without hesitation. My parents, Fred and Barb Southard, think this is cool, which I think is unusual and fantastic. My brothers, Gerrit and Tor, keep me laughing.

The third thank you is to those who have shaped my perspective on the art and craft of public speaking. I spent one year as a colleague of George LaMaster at Marian University, but that was the most formative year of my outlook on speech making and coaching. Melissa Franke, Brian Shipley, Kyle Hunsicker, and Brent Northup were great speech mentors and friends as I developed my own voice. Andrew Wolvin helped me understand how to translate presentation skills to the professional world, although I will never be as good at this as he is. And special thanks to Jane Berry-Eddings, my high school speech and debate coach, English teacher, and mentor.

The fourth and final thank you is to the students that I have worked with at Marian College, Lewis & Clark College, and University of Georgia. Thanks for listening to me and sharing your speeches.

Made in the USA
Columbia, SC
03 March 2019